HINDU WOMEN'S PROPERTY
RIGHTS IN RURAL INDIA

For all my family, especially Bapa, Ma and Manish

Hindu Women's Property Rights in Rural India

Law, Labour and Culture in Action

REENA PATEL
University of Warwick, UK

ASHGATE

Published by
Ashgate Publishing Limited
Gower House
Croft Road
Aldershot
Hampshire GU11 3HR
England

Ashgate Publishing Company
Suite 420
101 Cherry Street
Burlington, VT 05401-4405
USA

Ashgate website: http://www.ashgate.com

British Library Cataloguing in Publication Data
Patel, Reena
    Hindu women's property rights in rural India : law, labour
    and culture in action
    1. Right of property - India 2. Women peasants - Legal
    status, laws, etc. - India 3. Women's rights - India
    4. Women's rights - Religious aspects - Hinduism 5. Women -
    Legal status, laws, etc. (Hindu law) 6. Property (Hindu
    law) 7. Inheritance and succession (Hindu law)
    I. Title
    346.5'40432

Library of Congress Cataloging-in-Publication Data
Patel, Reena.
    Hindu women's property rights in rural India : law, labour and culture in action /
    by Reena Patel.
        p. cm.
    Includes bibliographical references and index.
    ISBN 978-0-7546-4616-7 (alk. paper)
        1. Women--Legal status, laws, etc. (Hindu law) 2. Women peasants--Legal status,
    laws, etc.--India. 3. Right of property--India. 4. Property (Hindu law) 5. Inheritance
    and succession (Hindu law) I. Title.

    KNS516.P38 2007
    346.5404'32--dc22
                                                                        2007000327

ISBN: 978-0-7546-4616-7

Printed and bound in Great Britain by Antony Rowe Ltd, Chippenham, Wiltshire.

Contents

Preface

I come to this project from a particular position. One part is rooted in the lives and experiences of my parents, who are both the children of farmers and whose kin (and therefore my own) network is that of a community of farmers. The stories which we grew up listening to were those based upon and woven around land, the seasons, crops and their life cycles. The spectre of 'work' that always remained to be done and given as a reply when we entreated visiting uncles and aunts to stay longer as children was bound by an urgency that was non-negotiable, much to our disappointment. The window of opportunity they worked around always seemed very small and the burden almost unmanageable – either it was the precise time for sowing (in anticipation of the rains) or the problem was transplanting (who was going to be drafted in to provide the many hands necessary?), weeding as soon as possible (or it would become unmanageable and ruin the crop) and on and on. It *never* seemed to a good time for my grandmother to take a few days off, no matter what time of the year.

Important events, crises and successes as well as normality were all framed within this life. To see the fire in the kitchen of my grandmother's house burning at all times, and almost always with a pot on it was a normal sight. To know that meals had to be prepared at all hours was normal, because all those hands helping with the weeding, transplanting or whatever, had to be fed in addition to the family. For a child, the rains seemed particularly troublesome. If it rained too little, it produced a crisis. But then, if it rained too much, that was another crisis and if it did not rain at all, it was also the time for sleepless nights for the adults. My parents' sense of emotional security and well-being were intimately tied to these events, and to that extent affected their children's sense of everything being well. This history of being part of a farming community, whose grandparents, uncles, aunts and practically every other relative lived in villages, and growing up with values that sustain this framework is one part of my position today.

The other, equally fundamental aspect is that of a woman who has been exposed to and benefited from education. Even though intimately part of the rural, farming setup of my wider family, my own parents were based in towns. No further than 100 km they may be from the village, but they were *towns*. Enmeshed as he was in the farming world as the only child of his farmer parents, my father himself was an engineer and civil servant. As such, he decided that farming could not be the backbone of his children's lives, and therefore had be educated. My education at excellent institutions in India placed me in a position quite unlike what could have been expected within my family's context. First of all, it placed me in a starkly different position to other girls from 'our' farming community. In a context where education was not predominant in sustaining the life-cycle and status of females, education for myself, a girl, gave me a wholly different position as compared to most other girls from the farming community. More fundamentally, it proved from the outset that no system of values is so entrenched as to be immutable and girls *could* be educated. Being educated and exposed to life, values, and possibilities of the non-farming world taught me that where many things are possible, anything is possible.

The latent defiance in this notion that structures may be negotiated and possibilities explored, *by/as a girl*, pose a threat to those in power. But that is precisely what education means to those who realize the privilege of receiving it. Education helps to sow the seeds of unmitigated agency in engaging with meanings and structures of power, of reshaping one's own choices, actions and surroundings and to that extent, reshaping one's destiny.

I am now based within an academic institution in the North/West. Being so privileged many times over, I hardly represent many of the women I write about, think about. Not only have I had the choices and chances to shape my own values and life to a large extent because of my education, I am now located within an intellectual, academic tradition that has not been very cognisant of its power to shape meanings, discourse, and ultimately power over women in the Developing World.

I am therefore, both an insider and an outsider to this project. I am an insider to the extent that I recognize, understand and empathize with values, structures and lives led by millions of women in farming communities, in villages in India. But I am an outsider in that I have not lived them myself, and have the privileged position to challenge and/or reject discriminating values and structures *regardless of any sanction*. I hope and believe, that as education has spread, this privilege is more of a right, and that more challenges to discriminatory values and structures will eventually reduce the gravity of the challenge and hence the sanctions to such challenges.

This book is about the choices that women, working on the land for cultivation, are presented with in relation to rights over land. It is about what values form part of our understanding of ourselves as women, and how these values lead to the construction of choices in often very limited terms. It is about the conflicts created by different sets of values in relation to any given rights, and how those conflicts present possible solutions.

This book is based upon women's realities, their experiences and perceptions as the necessary foundation for a deeper, contextual and critical engagement with law. Ann Oakley writes of doing research:

> ... as an essential way of giving the subjective situation of women greater visibility not only in Sociology but more importantly, in society, than it has traditionally had. Interviewing women was, then, a strategy for documenting women's own account of their lives... (Oakley, 1995, 40).

In exploring law as it relates to women, then, the need to develop an understanding of the specific, real ways in which women understand their locations within the various structures of society which inform the law is even greater. Uncovering what women understood/experienced and bringing women's voices into society is relevant and urgent where the norm places greater value on silence; here the very act of speaking is itself outside the norm, and even more so to speak of *one's own opinions as a woman*. Soliciting and encouraging women to express and voice their own opinions may itself be seen to be subversive of the dominant norm. In the context of the patriarchal structure of a society, with controls upon women coupled with the idealization of 'non-presence', silence reflects the ultimate condition of the absence of autonomy. I hope that the research process may have contributed to the women in some small way, towards initiating a process of greater control, starting with the identification and expression of their own interests.

Acknowledgements

I am especially grateful to all my sisters in Orissa who shared their time and thoughts with me on potentially sensitive issues. I thank them for their indulgence of my naïve ignorance of seemingly obvious explanations and for the trouble they took to explain their views to me. I am grateful to my colleagues at the University of Warwick for helping me through the many years of thinking, exploring, arguing and understanding. In particular, I am very indebted to my dear friends and colleagues Shirin Rai, Upendra Baxi and Shaheen Sardar Ali. Their support and generosity with their time and thoughts helped to deepen and sharpen my thoughts in those early days of my academic development. I also wish to thank Ann Stewart, my Doctoral supervisor, for all her help. My friends have been with me in this endeavour in myriad ways and I owe it to them for keeping my spirits and helping me, especially Shraddha Chigateri. Through the difficult years of trying to complete the research, I will always cherish the love and friendship of many loved ones and friends at Warwick.

I am extremely grateful to Prof. Werner F Menski for his time and thoughts on my work. His willingness to engage with my thoughts, very constructive comments and support for the book have been very precious. I also thank the anonymous reviewer for extremely helpful suggestions and contributions.

My family have been my support in innumerable ways. Jagyan Ma, Petu Dada, Bai and never the least, Budha Dada: you have been my inspiration in so many ways. Each of you taught me the possibilities of life, of being female and being independent and respected as an individual. I can never adequately express my admiration for what you achieved even in your time. This work is an offering to your richly lived lives. Manish, who has been my friend and absolute pillar of strength through so many years and many very difficult times, I thank for keeping me sane, not letting me give up and encouraging me every step of the way.

Finally, I would like to thank the Nuffield Foundation for financial assistance which made the field research possible.

Chapter 1

Introduction

Hindu women in India have independent right of ownership to property under the law of succession.[1] However, during the last five decades of its operation not many women have exercised their rights under the enactment (Sharma, 1989; Agarwal, 1994; Devi, 1994; Brown et al., 2002). This book studies the construction of Hindu women's claim to independent land ownership within law in India.

For the predominantly rural population in India with subsistence agriculture as the mainstay in conditions of poverty, land assumes significance as the subject of property. In the context of rural India, land was and continues to be the only viable resource for the production of food and meeting basic subsistence needs for a large part of the rural population. In response to this reality statutory provisions have been introduced since independence to address various issues regarding equitable land ownership and distribution. On the particular significance of independent property rights for greater overall empowerment and improvement of women's status within society, the Hindu Succession Act explicitly overcomes the traditional exclusion of Hindu women from inheriting ancestral property which is overwhelmingly in the form of land. Land therefore assumes a primary significance in any critical evaluation of law aimed ostensibly at enabling Hindu women's rights to property ownership.

The right of Hindu peasant women in small and marginal farming households to own property independently is the narrower focus of this book. In these households, the minimal size of landholdings precludes the use of hired labour, and production is carried out through the work of family members including women. In overall conditions of poverty, the nature of agriculture within these households may be characterized as subsistence production, and women's active labour participation is a significant factor in the households' agricultural production. The issues regarding rights of women in these households may be distinguished from landless agricultural labourers working on others' land. While the former work on the land owned by the family, the latter work on others' land for remuneration. As such, the major issue for female landless labourers in the context of ownership is the right to benefit equally from any land redistribution programmes to endow the landless. In the absence of effective and equal land redistribution programmes, the foremost issues for female landless labourers are the right to minimum wages from the employer and equal remuneration as men for equal work. As the means of property acquisition and ownership, inheritance and succession become relevant for women within peasant households with some landholdings. The issue does not arise for landless agricultural labourers, where property acquisition depends upon transfers by the state.

---

1   The Hindu Succession Act, 1956.

The right to acquire land through inheritance and succession within the rural context is significant for a number of reasons. First, the overwhelming dependence on agriculture as the means of survival makes land the most viable resource for all those depending upon it. In the absence of a social security net (Guhan, 1992), ownership of land is therefore vital to overcome dependence upon others for survival and for the fulfilment of vital subsistence needs However, land markets in rural India are severely constrained due to the nature of subsistence production and limited potential for cash transactions. Further, the socio-cultural and political implications of land ownership, and the popular belief that the possession of land leads to power and prestige, results in low levels of land sales (Basu, 1990; Shah, 1993; Jacobs, 1996). Succession is therefore the primary means of acquisition of land where the above factors do not readily allow for the acquisition of land through the conversion of other forms of property.[2]

The discussion in this book addresses the issue of Hindu peasant women's ability to translate their statutory rights to succession into practice and assert ownership of their share in family land. It is based upon a critical analysis of law to highlight the significance of the socio-cultural and ideological context of legal rights and entitlements. In exploring the specific implications for gender based rights and entitlements, the discussion engages with recent feminist analyses of gender and the allocation of resources within the household/family. It highlights the ideological foundations of the existing legal right and explores the implications of including an analysis of the material factors affecting women's effective claim to land. Within the specific framework of the Hindu Succession Act, it proposes that whereas law constructs such a claim as a *right*, addressed to *Hindu* women, located within the *family* and predicated upon *religious ideology*, it should include a consideration of women's *interests* in land ownership as *peasants*, within the *household* and as affected by their *work and contributions*. Such a construction based upon women's interests, would enable a more critical evaluation of legal entitlements currently formulated upon a particular subjectivity of women as 'Hindu'.

The work of many scholars on the interactions between gender, society and property in the Indian context has irrefutably established that women's status, as determined by both the material and ideological structures within society, is crucial both to our understanding of women's exclusion and for evolving possibilities for change. Analysis of access to resources, and land in particular, has highlighted the need to take account of gender relations operating at various levels in society, and impacting upon women in specific ways (Agarwal, 1995, 1994; Moore, 1995; Jacobs,

---

2   In the global context, the focus of land rights debates addressed the parameters of state transfers of land through private/community control and the gender dimensions of such transfers. Although issues of inter-generational transfers through inheritance and succession, do not necessarily form the focus at this time, and do not assume the same importance for gender equality and access elsewhere as they do in India, they remain implicitly fundamental in the consideration of the continuity of policy reforms through state transfers. For an excellent discussion of the need to locate discussions of 'land rights' within specific historical, political, economic, legal and developmental contexts, see Razavi (2003).

2002).[3] The 'bargaining approach'[4] has been particularly useful in highlighting the impact of factors such as gender, status and class upon the distribution of resources among individual members of a group such as the family, household or community. It has also enabled an understanding of the processes involved in such distribution, whether, for example, they are co-operative or conflictual. Adopting this, the interactions between the various members are conceived of as negotiations involving both co-operation and conflict, where the outcome of negotiations would depend upon the relative bargaining position of the members. This conception is particularly useful in analysing resource distribution within the household, bringing into question the previously held belief that household distribution of resources is based upon total harmony, resulting from altruism, love and affection. The works of Amartya Sen and Bina Agarwal are especially significant for their contribution to the development of this analysis, particularly in the context of South Asia.

The works of Sen (1983, 1987, 1990) on the impact of gender upon access to resources through negotiation and bargaining, and Agarwal's application of this in relation to women and land ownership in India provide the conceptual basis for this book. Sen's framework elaborates upon the bargaining approach to take account of perceptions affecting the legitimacy of the claim.[5] According to this, legitimacy is affected by (the person's) perceptions of self-interest and (others') perceptions of the value of her contributions. Sen places importance on perceptions of self-interest in enabling a greater social legitimacy for their claim and therefore a stronger bargaining position for land. He goes on to argue that women's individual self-interest may often be lacking and needs to be enhanced, particularly in traditional societies like India.

Agarwal (1994) who provides a rich and detailed analysis of the position of women in relation to independent land ownership in the context of existing normative and institutional factors adopts and extends Sen's analysis. However, she contests his conceptualization of and importance given to 'self-interest' in determining women's welfare as the outcome of bargaining. Further, she disagrees with Sen's proposition that women in traditional societies (such as India) tend to have a less sharp perception of their individual interests and argues that, 'what may be needed is less a sharpening of women's sense of self-interest, than an improvement in their ability to pursue that interest' (Agarwal, 1994, 57). Thus, she argues that women's self-interest is clearly defined, even in traditional societies such as India. Moreover, that the focus needs to be upon creating and establishing the frameworks to uphold women's self-interest, rather than upon what that interest encompasses. In addition to the social legitimacy

---

3   See Jackson (2003) for a thesis questioning whether land rights for women have the transformative potential for gender relations that may ideally be hoped for.

4   The bargaining 'approach' as distinct from the bargaining 'model' is a development that enables the adoption of the 'model'. While the 'model' is based upon economic theoretic formulations of the various factors and outcomes and their relationship *inter se*, the bargaining 'approach' is broader, enabling a perspective based upon the incorporation of the principles.

5   The components of the bargaining approach as developed by Sen and extended further by Agarwal are discussed in detail in the following chapter.

of the claim and women's access to economic and social resources outside the existing support systems, law is one of the factors that would determine women's ability to bargain for land (Agarwal, 1994, 66). Whereas existing laws regarding ownership of land by women are relevant for establishing the legal legitimacy of the claim, women's knowledge of their rights and access to legal machinery and public bodies administering land are significant for effective access.

The development of the bargaining approach enables clearer analyses of resource allocation and distribution among individuals within a group. Within the family, in particular, it allows for the evaluation of social and cultural factors as they determine economic positioning. In the particular analysis of gender as it impacts upon bargaining, the role of tradition and cultural ideology can be seen to be significant in affecting material equality. The need to take account of cultural and ideological gender bias in elucidating inequalities in access to resources is thus clearly brought out by the bargaining approach.

This book develops the bargaining approach from a legal perspective to engage in a critical evaluation of the social and economic context of law. It is an exploration of the existing legal framework in India as it operates to impact upon Hindu peasant women's ability to negotiate access to land. It argues that the existing formulation of women's right to land within regimes of religious law asserts a monolithic construction both of women's identities as well as their interests. Such a law denies the existence of women's subjective identification with the role of peasant and worker in addition to that of being Hindu women. The simultaneously multiple and intersecting identities of women as Hindu, individual, wife, worker, mother or other are completely overlooked by this simplistic and ultimately problematic, construction within law. A law which does not account for the varying and complex subject positions misleads in its account of what it has legitimated. It obscures the inherent conflict we each embody to the extent that different values and aims inform different aspects of our subjectivity. It further obscures the problem of making choices and resolving the inherent conflicts in pursuing our lives.

An approach which analyses and critiques law 'from within and below' needs necessarily to account for the competing claims and interests to which an individual is subject. Bargaining and negotiation are integral to these final 'choices' or resolutions which we as individuals make. The view of law from such a subject-orientated perspective is not one of a coherent, single value system, but a complex and often contradictory mix of values. As Sinha, speaking of a polycentric approach to law suggests:

> We face conflicting values both in personal life and in the community life. It is an inaccurate representation of common life experience to suggest that these conflicting values are reconcilable under one truth, rather than poised for bargaining and give-and-take, that they are resolved into one absolute, rather than subject to multiple evaluations and multiple judgements in the context of their contingent factors … (1995: 44).

The specific social, religious and material context of Hindu peasant women are probed in this study to generate a deeper understanding of their concrete, lived realities and the choices generated therefrom. While enabling a clearer analysis of

Hindu women's constraints and powers in making choices affecting their ownership of land, the bargaining approach contributes towards furthering the study of law in its social context through a critical analysis of the guaranteed legal rights which frame such choices.

By critically evaluating the significance of religious and traditional norms, which are in opposition to the rights established by law, this book seeks to further the discussion of Hindu law within the broader constitutional framework. The specific issue of women's right to own property under the law of succession provides the basis to further the understanding of Hindu law as it operates upon women 'on the ground'. Addressing the development of the contemporary legal framework as the culmination of the processes, debates and dominant values of the state and society preceding independence, the analysis of the law in relation to Hindu succession reveals the close interaction and continuation of pre-colonial, colonial and post-colonial law.

The discussion and analysis in this book have been drawn from field research conducted in Western Orissa. This research was conducted in three villages in the period 1995–1998. Based upon discussions with Hindu peasant women from small and marginal farming households, it builds upon their perceptions of the ideological foundations of Hindu women's exclusion from property, and the inexorable links between gender identity, religious ideology and land ownership in their lives.

The Research Setting: Asking the Questions and Identifying the Issues

Field research was conducted in the villages of Sahaspur, Ekatali and Karamdihi in the two western districts of Sundargarh and Jharsuguda in Orissa. These are bordered by Madhya Pradesh on the west and Bihar in the north. This region can be distinguished from the rest of Orissa geographically, linguistically, culturally and even economically. My affinity and familiarity with the region made this area a natural choice to conduct my research. Generations of my family have been residents within the area and I myself have lived in the area as a result of my parents' location there. My wider family also live in the area and we are part of a kinship and caste structure that is predominantly located in this geographical region. These districts in particular are predominantly rural, far out balancing the urban areas both in organization and population. Females constitute an overwhelming proportion of marginal workers and conversely, a disproportionately small number of main workers. Although women constitute an insignificant group among cultivators, their numbers grow substantially in proportion to male agricultural labourers.

The people in the districts speak a dialect of Oriya, known as 'Sambalpuri Oriya',[6] which is prevalent throughout the region. This differs from the Oriya which is spoken in the coastal and other districts of Orissa, and also spoken by a number

---

6   Named after the neighbouring district of Sambalpur, which became part of Orissa in 1936, on the basis that Oriya was the language of the area. Previously, under the administration of the central provinces, Sambalpur was transferred to the Orissa division of the province of Bengal on the recognition that Oriya, and not Hindi, was the mother tongue of the people (Gazetteer, 1971, 79).

of people in the adjacent districts of Madhya Pradesh such as Raipur, Raigarh and Surguja. The dialect has a different mode of pronunciation as well as grammatical structure, and contains a large vocabulary which is not a part of the official Oriya language. The official Oriya language, it may be pointed out, is that spoken by the people in the coastal and other areas. Although many refer to Sambalpuri Oriya as a dialect, it is distinctly different from the official Oriya.

The research was conducted partly through discussions with a total of 42 women from three villages: Sahaspur, Karamdihi and Ekatali. Drawn from landowning castes and labourers, with predominantly small and marginal landholdings, participants included both married and unmarried women aged between 20 and 66 years. It was important to draw participants from this wider group towards exploring the link, if any, between the legitimacy of women's claim, their culturally constructed gender roles and their work contribution in cultivation. The contribution of women's work to household production is generally most significant among marginal landholding households. Here, the landholdings are generally not large enough to require hired labour and moreover, the family income of such households is not large enough to pay for hired labour.

Ranging around the key issues for consideration, discussions were held with participants in groups and based upon reflexive interviewing, using mainly non-directive questions and a few directive questions. This was a productive method for eliciting participants' views and opinions to the maximum possible extent. The issue of women's right to inherit property was addressed through a discussion of related questions including: (a) the legitimacy or otherwise of women's claim to land ownership and the basis of such legitimacy; (b) the effect of a legal change upon the question of legitimacy of women's claim; (c) the willingness of participants to enforce their legal right to parental property and reasons for the same; (d) willingness of participants to claim a share of husband's property and reasons for the same. On the link between legitimacy, work contributions and land ownership, relevant issues which were discussed included: (a) the enumeration of 'work' by women; (b) women's evaluation of their own work in comparison with that of male family members; (c) others' evaluation of their work, as perceived by the women themselves; (d) entitlements/privileges, if any, resulting from work roles and contribution; and (e) the link, if any, between legitimate property rights and work contribution.

Access and Interaction: Between 'Insider' and 'Outsider'

I was privileged to have relatively easy access to the women. My position was privileged in that I am a member of the *Agharia*[7] sub-caste, and therefore prima facie, not an 'outsider' for many of the women who were of the same caste. In two of the villages, many women with whom I had discussions were related kin, given that within a relatively small caste group such as the *Agharias*, 'everybody can

---

7   This is the predominant agricultural group in the area. Although relatively low in the traditional caste hierarchy, they are nevertheless among the more powerful groups due to the fact that they are usually landholders of small and medium farms and do not usually engage in wage labour on others' farms.

be traced as being a relative of somebody else'. Researchers have written of how they, as female researchers, obtained access to the field through the connections and position of their male relatives (Gupta, 1979; Abu-Lughod, 1993; Berik, 1996). In my case, interestingly, the 'gatekeepers' were all females, and it was my relationship to them that enabled me to gain access. It was the reputation and influence hitherto wielded by my grandmothers and their immediate family that allowed me access as a researcher.

Although, as I have said earlier, I was known to many of the women as a member of the *Agharia* caste and was an 'insider' in that sense, I was also in many ways an 'outsider' who represented much that they could not share through their experiences. I represented unusual independence for a female given that I had lived outside the physical guardianship of my parents in 'foreign' places from a very young age ('foreign' here is equivalent to its normal meaning, although it extends to distant places, not necessarily only those crossing national boundaries). My fluency in English was evidence of a very exclusive and privileged education, also representing a significant exposure to Western culture[8] and values, which are in turn alien to theirs. This was perhaps substantiated, in their eyes, by the fact that I was unmarried even at the age of 25, wore 'Western' attire such as trousers and skirts, had my hair cut short and was not particularly deferential in attitude, to name but a few aberrations. As caste networks operate, this meant that almost all of the women knew of me, as 'so-and-so's daughter' 'doing such-and-such', that made me 'different' / 'modern' / 'foreign' and 'not really one of them'.

While many have brought out the limitations imposed upon and faced by foreign women in doing field research, particularly in Middle East and the South (Pettigrew, 1988; Kumar, 1992), in my experience my 'otherness' gave me the freedom to do what I had to do. My lack of conformity in terms of dress, role, interactions and work as a 'student' researcher were, I found, tolerated and even indulged by many in the villages. Wolf (1996) refers to this aspect, that whereas she expected the villagers in her study to be scandalized by her personal situation, they were in fact 'delighted rather than scandalised'. The interaction was based not only on my otherness, but most importantly, my being different gave me freedom only because I was taken to be first and foremost, one of them. *Jati*[9] affiliation was the primary binding factor, upon which the differences in class background could operate. I was very conscious of these differences since, as my own previous experience of growing up in that context had shown on many occasions, external markers of 'difference' can minimize the scope for identity of interests based upon gender. However, I found that the differences were taken as a given by the women. Moreover, it was because of their knowledge that I could not fully understand their

---

8 This becomes clearer if one takes into account the fact that most English medium schools till recently were in fact run by foreign missionaries. Being a residential student, as I was, therefore meant an even greater exposure and inculcation of their culture, social ways and behaviour.

9 This is the term for sub-caste, which is in fact the operative 'caste' in Indian society. It connotes affiliation to the community not only on the basis of membership, but where it is small, approximated kinship as well.

lives, that they embarked upon discussions, which were seen by them as a chance to enlighten me. In what could be seen as a reversal of the power relations in the research process, *they* were telling *me*, because I was ignorant, and they were telling *me* because I was one of them in terms of the extensions of the family that often denoted the *Jati*.

In addition to *Jati* the importance of being able to speak the local language, *Sambalpuri* and *Agharia* in conducting my research was crucial. While *Jati* enabled to a great extent the women's initial agreement to enter into an interaction with me, the interaction itself became a meaningful one by virtue of the language. In this situation, it was my knowledge of their language and my ability to communicate with them using their own expressions and in their terms that really gave me their acceptance and affinity to share their thoughts and ideas with me and their trust to allow my probing into their personal opinions. While my family status and personal qualification gave me access, the intimidation this might have produced was possibly reduced by my knowledge of their language.

I should note here that the *Agharia* language is considered by many to be rustic and in many instances is replaced by Oriya as a result of upward social mobility. The migration and relocation of families in urban areas produces a similar effect where the language is no longer in use. Language as an aspect of identity was clear in the questions and comments of many women expressing their pleased surprise at my knowledge of it, pride that I had not discarded it, and implicit acceptance. My sharing of the language re-established my identity as 'one of them' although this process was within the context of interactions with me as a researcher.

My *Jati* membership also allowed me to gain access to the group of *Kisan* women. As labourers, these women were generally hired by an *Agharia* large landholding family in the village and also worked for *Agharia* households as domestic helpers. Thus, I gained access to these women as a 'relative' of those who provided their employment. In this case, my role as a researcher would have been completely as an outsider, were it not for the commonality of language and gender. In this case, the class and power connotations are clear, and I am aware that my 'higher' position may have implicitly compelled the women to allow me access, at the same time that their actual participation and responses in the discussion may have been a constrained one. Further, in both situations my qualification as a lawyer gave me a position both of authority and a point of seeking informal advice. Nevertheless, my family background, language ability and caste affiliation allowed me access to have discussions with the women as freely as I did to successfully complete the research.

Organization of Chapters

The framework of analysis upon which the book builds, explaining the components of the bargaining approach, and discussing its relevance for a gendered analysis of access to resources is discussed in Chapter 2. In particular, I highlight conceptualizations of the household that it has enabled. The bargaining approach has made prior assumptions about the unitary nature of the household problematic, that it is characterized by a singularity of interests among all its members, represented by its head. It questions the assumption derived from a unitary conception of interests, that altruism thereafter dictates the equitable distribution of the resources among various members by the head. Rather, the bargaining approach conceives of the household as comprised of a plurality of interests of individual members, where the allocation of resources is not presumed as flowing out of altruism, but as a result of negotiation between the members.

The bargaining approach has also provided a framework for taking account of women's work and contribution in analyses of resource allocation and distribution. Within this, the recognition accorded to women's work is brought into focus as a determinant of their access to resources. I discuss the issues that are particularly relevant to women working in household production and subsistence agriculture. In these contexts, the recognition of women's work has been shown to be highly problematic. At the same time, the non-recognition of women's work has been shown to be a contributory factor in women's exclusion from access to resources.

The above issues raised in regard to developing gendered analysis of access to resources by the bargaining approach provide the basis for a critical evaluation of the legal framework. I discuss the problems implicit within the liberal constitutional and legal framework in India from the perspective of addressing gender inequality. The assumptions of equality and neutrality within the liberal framework are discussed as problematic. In particular, these assumptions obscure the implicit location of the female within a subordinate status. I discuss these aspects of the law as they determine issues within the particular laws that regulate women's right to property. Further, in the specific Indian context, the history of its development through the colonial period and after raises questions about the particular direction of law in relation to gender equality. In particular, the inability of law to move beyond the colonial discourse predicated upon religion is discussed in relation to instituting rights within personal law.

In Chapter 3 I discuss the provisions of the Hindu Succession Act (1956) (hereinafter referred to as HSA) as part of the historical development of Hindu women's legal right to property ownership. This chapter discusses the regulation of women's property rights within classical or traditional Hindu law and the changes gradually sought to be introduced by legislation. Indian legal history includes thousands of years of indigenous rule, during which evolved highly developed rules of conduct, administration of justice and government. Following this, the greatest impact upon the legal system in terms of the development of rules and institutions for the administration of justice came from the colonial experience. Post-independence India is marked by the adoption of the Constitution of India in 1950, providing the fundamental principles and framework in accordance with which all subsequent legal development must take form. The chapter discusses the impact of colonial administration in the codification of Hindu women's rights, and its subsequent form and content in the post-colonial constitutional framework. A critical evaluation of the HSA brings out inconsistencies among its provisions regarding women's right to acquire property.

The clarity with which women analyse their own experiences as 'Hindu' women within peasant households with marginal landholdings is revealing and demands recognition. Chapter 4 presents women's own analysis of gender within their context, the role of cultural and religious ideology in determining gender relations and the impact of these upon their access and ownership to land. On the issue of right to land ownership, it explores their perceptions of legitimacy and explores notions of self-interest to acquire land through succession and inheritance. It brings out the crucially important divergence between their own perceptions and valuations of their work and others' perceptions of their work and contributions within their households.

In Chapter 5 I evaluate Hindu women's self-interest in acquiring a share in parental property through succession, which is the objective of the statutory enactments discussed in Chapter 3. Based upon the close engagement of statutory law to Hindu religious principles discussed in that chapter, I evaluate specific aspects relating to women's position within Hindu principles as they might impact upon their right to land ownership. I do this through a discussion of their roles as wives, widows and daughters. Starting with references to these roles as discussed in ancient Hindu literature, I show their contemporary applications in decisions by courts and their resonance in contemporary society. I thereafter discuss the implicit as well as explicit assumptions upon which the legal changes incorporating Hindu women's rights to property were based. I evaluate the extent to which these assumptions are borne out, and the extent to which the law reflects and strengthens Hindu women's self-interest.

The issue of work contributions as it affects women's claim to land ownership is discussed in Chapter 6. Progressing from the evaluation of the religious and ideological context of law in Chapter 5, I discuss the material context of Hindu peasant women as agricultural workers and producers. The nature, extent and role of their contribution in household and subsistence agriculture are discussed. I highlight the problems that arise in the context of women's work, particularly within household and subsistence production. These include problems with defining women's work, non-recognition leading to under-enumeration and the resulting persistent under-valuation. The ideological basis of such under-valuation is explored, where gender-biased ideology itself may be determinative of the low value placed on women's work and contribution. This chapter takes the example of land reforms in India as an example of the law's failure to take account of women's work and contribution to agricultural production. The case of land reforms, which were premised upon work contribution as creating the basis for land ownership for those who had been historically excluded, is presented as a reflection of the issues regarding women's role in agriculture. Its failure to take particular account of women presents an example of the outcome of the persistent under-valuation of women's work. The chapter discusses this failure within land reforms as it excludes women's ownership of land on the basis of their role and contribution, and argues that in doing so, fails to strengthen their claim to land ownership.

Throughout this book, I explore the impact of gender relations upon legal guarantees and entitlements. In the specific context of Hindu peasant women in small farming households, such impact is determined both by the ideological context of Hindu society, and within the material context of peasant women's role work and contribution in agriculture. The legal efforts to enact statutory rights to succession through the Act reflect an attempt to redress the material (non) relation of Hindu females to land through ownership, where such absence of ownership is an aspect of gender relations within the society. Whereas women in rural areas are primarily engaged, to various extents, as *workers* in agricultural production, the issue that has been addressed by statutory enactment, but which remains and is discussed here, is of establishing *ownership* as the basis of women's relation to land. It addresses Hindu women's claim to land ownership through a study of their particular experience of gender within Hindu society and family, as well as their particular location within agricultural production in rural areas.

Chapter 2

A Conceptual Map

Introduction

This chapter identifies the particular issues that arise in conceptualizing Hindu women's access to land within small farming households, developed and addressed through field research in rural Western Orissa. As noted earlier, such access is primarily established by the HSA, which confers upon Hindu women the right to claim a share to property through succession.

The regime set up by the HSA is located within the broader constitutional and legal framework existing in India today. In order to evaluate the factors that affect Hindu women's ability to exercise their rights, two fundamental aspects of this broader legal framework will be examined. The historically constructed role of tradition and modernity within the Constitutional (and derivative legal) framework, and the liberal foundation of this framework have a critical bearing upon how Hindu women's right to property is constructed by law.

Religion provides the ideological framework for the constitution of 'Hindu' law such as the HSA, within which the role of 'tradition' has particular implications for women. Whereas a major impetus for various progressive legislations, including the HSA, was the establishment of 'modern' values such as equality, the construction of this 'modernity' is itself a product of colonial engagement. In the context of the historical and developmental trajectory of post – independence legal framework in India, where an opposition between 'modernity' and 'tradition' is deeply embedded, the need to reconcile these established religion as the legitimizing principle. The existence of contemporary 'Hindu law' reflects the continued hegemony of religion, and within it, of tradition.

Notwithstanding guarantees of formal equality, the liberal principles embodied in the Constitution reinforce the reality of women's substantive inequality in two ways. First, the public/private distinction within liberal principles predicates the exclusion of formal law from the 'family' or the home. This operates to strengthen the role of religion and tradition in the regulation of women, which functions predominantly within the family. Secondly, the exclusion of the family from law's purview, and the ideological construction of women's lives within it, results in the exclusion of the related but separate sphere of the household, its constitutive relations and women's lives within the household.

Insights provided by studies into legal pluralism enable a broader focus in the discussion of the way in which women's lives are affected by law. The study of law in its broader context necessitates taking into account women's lived realities, and the analysis of the material and ideological processes and structures by which they are constituted. The bargaining approach is useful for analyses of gender and access to resources by establishing the relevance of the material processes and structures, in addition to ideologically derived constructions, which form the totality of women's lives. Whereas the legal framework structures Hindu women's claim to property as a *right*, addressed to *Hindu* women, located in the *family* and predicated upon (religion-based) ideology, it must include women's claim to property as founded upon their *interest*, as *peasant women*, located within the *household* and predicated upon their material conditions of work and production.

The Framework of Law

To evaluate the role of law in establishing effective property rights for women, it is necessary to specify what one means by 'law' within the analysis. Law may be conceptualized and evaluated in various ways and at various levels, given its very nature and ability to operate as a social system in society as well as prescribe and enforce norms of behaviour. Law may therefore be 'both a prescriptive norm and a descriptive fact' (Cotterell, 1992, 8). Moreover, law may be studied within its own terms and with reference to its own conceptions, as legal positivists would argue, or it may be addressed and evaluated in relation to the social structure within which it operates (Cotterell, 1992; Ross, 2001).

The scope of what we mean by 'law' and the functions it serves as such, are therefore a precursor to any evaluation, critical or otherwise, of 'law' within a given problem, society or other context. Regarding the particular problem of Hindu peasant women's land ownership within the broader legal and political context of the Indian state, the starting point of this discussion is of law as prescriptive norms, embodied in rules, statutes and the constitutional framework, as well judicial pronouncements on these. It is necessary to evaluate the expressed aims which this law seeks to fulfil, drawing upon and engaging with analyses where law is discussed not in terms of individual rules and institutions, but as a social system in and of itself (Baxi, 1986; Posner, 2001). In this regard, the existence of a plurality of legal systems, sustained by the operation of religion and culture through social structures, has consequences for an analysis of law defined in its scope and functions as formal and positive.

Finally, the possibility of addressing gender concerns through law is explored and discussed through the inclusion of women's actual experiences and lived realities, in broadening the scope of a critical evaluation of law. The inclusion of women's social, material and ideological realities within a discussion of law, even as narrowly defined as above, enables a critique of the broader legal and political paradigms within which the state and constitution are framed, as well as the individual legal rules themselves.

The Constitutional Paradigm: 'Liberal' and 'Modern'

The law creates a dichotomy in constructing a woman's claim to land. This dichotomy is in constructing women's claim to land as a 'right', addressed to a 'Hindu women' located within the 'family' and framed by religious ideology, as opposed to addressing their 'interests', as 'peasant women', located within the 'household' and informed by their condition of work and production. The following discussion of law addresses the construction of Hindu women's right to property by succession (located within the first half of the dichotomy). I suggest that the liberal Constitutional framework and the derivative legislations both creates this dichotomy and locates women within the confines of the family and religious ideology in its determination of their claim to land as a 'right' through succession. The construction of women's claim within family or the private domain, it is argued, is embedded in the liberal framework of law to which considerations of 'Hindu' ideology and identity are added. Law's incorporation of 'Hindu' structures is founded upon the particular historical processes through which it evolved. The consequent retention of religion, and 'Hindu' as a principle of construction within law is discussed as it completes law's construction of women's claim to land as a right within the family, addressed to a Hindu women, and informed by Hindu religious ideology. Thus, law's 'liberal' character as well as its engagement with 'modernity' and 'tradition', taken together, demonstrate the process by which law both constructs and sustains a dichotomy, in framing women's claim to land, as well as locating women and their claim to land within one 'half' of this dichotomy.

The Indian Constitution is the embodiment of the avowed values, aims and objectives of the state after independence. It is a normative document, explicit in its vision of the society it seeks to foster. At the same time, it is a highly detailed document of the means and processes to be adopted in establishing such a society (making it the longest written constitution in the world).[1] As such, it provides a clear statement of the vision and modalities of the post-colonial state. 'As a post-colonial state, the Indian state occupies a particular space within the society and economy' (Rai, 1999, 241–242). Within this, the Constitution, and the legal framework it supports, is a relevant starting point for analyses of law and state in contemporary, post-colonial India. Indeed, as the Report of the Committee on the Status of Women notes, the role of law is highlighted in post-colonial states:

> The tasks of social reconstruction, development and nation building all call for major changes in the social order, to achieve which legislation is one of the main instruments. It can act directly, as a norm setter, or indirectly, providing institutions which accelerate social change by making it more acceptable (Committee on the Status of Women, 1975, 102).

The role of the post-colonial state is implicit in this understanding; it is conceived as different from that of the colonial administration in the way that the state addresses the citizens or subjects. While the colonial administration could not be presumed to be acting in the interests of the people, the nationalist debates and the independence

---

1   Nussbaum's development of the capabilities approach in the context of the Indian Constitution acknowledges this normative model incorporating values to be actively pursued by the state involving 'affirmative material and institutional support, not simply a failure to impede'. As she puts it, fundamental entitlements addressed to lower castes and women are 'not only not incompatible with constitutional guarantees, but are actually in their spirit' (Nussbaum, 2003, 38–39).

movement culminated in a Constitution that expresses the congruence of state and citizens' interests in the unequivocal 'We the People of India ....'[2] Thus, the presumption in contemporary Indian society is that the means and institution of the state are aimed towards, and reflective of, the will and desires of the Indian people, or at least the majority of them. While the colonial period is seen as being indifferent to 'humanitarian concerns' and 'social demands', it was the nationalist movement prior to independence, and the independent state thereafter, within which reforms have been possible.[3]

Undeniably, this is based upon the understanding of law as an instrument of social change, as has been the predominant focus of those engaging with law in India to address a whole range of social concerns, including those relating to gender. Kapur and Cossman question this reliance upon law as social engineering, particularly the assumptions made within this of the positive role of law in advancing women's equality and full participation (Kapur and Cossman, 1996). Although the limitations of law in bringing about social change is acknowledged, the reliance upon law as a means for bringing about social change:

> ... does not question law's commitment to social change, nor does it consider the role of law in the subordination of women .... It does not interrogate the ideological character of law in constituting and sustaining unequal power relations beyond the liberal understanding of explicitly discriminating laws. Rather, its focus is on law reform and law enforcement (Kapur and Cossman, 1996, 25).

Whereas the constitutional framework provides the overall justification for these engagements with law reform, an understanding of the framework makes clear the tensions within itself. In particular, the liberal framework that the Constitution adopts sits uncomfortably with simultaneous state led initiatives to redress structural and historical inequality of various groups, among them women. Secondly, the desire to create a 'New' India continues to have difficulty, that is, to what extent and in which areas it should break with 'India' as of old. These tensions are most clearly borne out in relation to state action through laws and institutions, in respect of the historically disadvantaged groups whom they are meant to address (Galanter, 1984; Menon, 1995).

Liberalism in Practice: The Feminist Critique

The Constitution of India sets out to integrate women into a full, democratic citizenship, through specific provisions[4] towards their equality and empowerment. The benevolence, egalitarianism and protection afforded by the Constitutional framework may be argued to mask the true nature of the state and law in respect of women, as a paternalistic one. Kapur and Cossman have argued that this is indeed so in the case of India (Kapur and Cossman, 1996). They have noted instances where

---

2   The Preamble, Constitution of India, 1950.
3   Status of Women in India (1988).
4   Provisions within the Fundamental Rights Chapter and the Directive Principles of State Policy.

the emphasis has been for the law to 'protect' women as the 'weaker sex', and argue that:

> This protectionist approach simply accepts traditional and patriarchal discourses that construct women as weak, biologically inferior, modest and so on ... the role of law is unproblematically asserted as protecting women. Laws that continue to treat women differently than men are accepted as a necessary part of this protection ... women's ostensibly natural differences are deployed to justify any differential treatment in law, and in effect, operate to preclude any entitlement to equality (Kapur and Cossman, 1996, 23).

Feminist critiques of liberalism have challenged the fundamental liberal principles of rationality and autonomy of the 'individual', the limitation of the power of the state and the consequent presumption of equality among all 'individuals' (Tong, 1998; Richardson, 2004). Pateman argues that in order to address gender equality and empowerment through law, it is not enough just to extend the concepts and arguments to women as well as men. It is necessary to rethink the concept of the individual (Pateman, 1986, 1988). Smart discusses the various ways that the liberal framework of the 'modern' state, of which law is an instrument, simply does not and can not allow for action towards gender equality and empowerment (Smart, 1984, 1989). Although the various strands of feminist thought may differ in the ways they understand and explain the relation of women to the state, they all agree that exclusion is a significant aspect of it. The focus on the individual is based upon the assumption of an abstraction: a concept free of the characteristics of gender, class, race and age (Naffine and Owens, 1997). This conception of an abstract, universal subject has been problematized and argued that it is sex/gender specific, affected by other factors of class, and so on (Siim, 1988; Lacey, 1997; O'Donovan, 1997).

Moreover, the concept of rationality is based upon assumptions of binary opposites within which the male and female were constructed including a distinction between body/mind, nature/culture, emotion/reason and so on. A central tenet of the liberal state has been the limitation of its action upon individuals, and certain areas where it should not act, where it is not its (or the law's) business (Barnett, 1998; Nussbaum, 2003). The public/private divide is based upon this, where:

> Public may be used to denote state activity, the values of the marketplace, work, the male domain or that sphere of activity that is regulated by the law. *Private* may denote civil society, the values of the family, intimacy, the personal life, home, the women's domain or behaviour unregulated by law (O'Donovan, 1985, 3).

As Jones has argued, the demarcation of the 'public' as fundamentally distinct from the 'private' resulted in women's exclusion from public life (Jones, 1988). Further, the distinction drawn between the male and female attributes combined with the demarcation of state action in the public/private realm to justify women's subordination in the private sphere:

> Hierarchical, patriarchal relations were held to be the natural characteristics of rule in the private sphere (Jones, 1988, 13).

The problem, however, was not in making the distinctions alone, it was the correspondence assumed with the distinction between male/female. Further, there was a value placed on the male as superior and female as inferior, and difficulty arises when positive or negative labels are attached to these attributes, particularly when it is that negative values attach to those associated with the female. Bottomley et al. point out that feminists of varying persuasions argue about how this should be addressed[5] (Bottomley et al., 1987). However, there is general agreement that the primary distinction between male/female and its correspondence to public/private within liberal thought is highly problematic for women.

Freeman suggests that the public/private dichotomy is at the heart of a critical approach to family law (Freeman, 1985). The public/private division has the same relation as a number of other oppositions which:

> ... taken together, constitute the liberal way of thinking about the social world. These distinctions are state/society, public/private, individual/group, right/power, property/ sovereignty, contract/tort, law/policy, legislature/judiciary, objective/subjective, reason/ fiat, freedom/coercion ... (Rose, 1987, 63).

This contradictory position between the ideals of individual freedom and equality in the public sphere, and the assumption that women are naturally subject to men in the family, argues Pateman, is the reason for the state's inability to address women's concerns (Pateman, 1986, 1988; Siim, 1988). Feminist critique has challenged not only the exclusion of the private from law and the state based upon the construction of public and private (O'Donovan, 1985; Pateman, 1986, 1988), but has also shown the linkages between the two spheres which continue to be unrecognized by the state and law (Bennholdt-Thomsen, 1981; Mackintosh, 1981)

Although Rose (1987) has called for analysis that goes beyond the public/ private debate, I believe that this analysis still has insights to offer us in attempts at a deeper understanding of law in India. Chatterjee offers such an insight in his discussion of the resolution of the 'woman question' within the nationalist discourse of pre-independent Indian society. He argues that the inner/outer dichotomy was an ideologically more powerful extension of the spiritual/material divide within nationalist discourse. This in turn translated into a world/home split where the woman was placed firmly within the home. The impact of this was to contribute to a particular construction of womanhood, with certain qualities and responsibilities, and upon which construction they could participate in the movement (Chatterjee, 1990).

The ramifications of the public/private divide may be seen in state reluctance to remove religion as the principle for personal (family) law (Mukhopadhyay, 1994; Narain, 2001).[6] It may also be seen in the reluctance to put into effect a Uniform Civil Code (Parasher, 1992, 1997; Agarwala and Ramanamma, 1994; Jaisingh,

---

5   The cultural feminists, such as Carol Gilligan and Luce Irigaray, for example, would argue for the superiority of the 'female' attributes, whereas others have argued that these oppositions are not valid in the first place.

6   For an illuminating, thorough and contextual critique of the processes of law and politics in relation to Muslim women in India, see further Narain (2001).

1996), although it is a Directive Principle of State Policy, and one which the state had undertaken a specific commitment to pass (Baxi, 1986). Further as will be discussed later, the legal reform of Hindu family law shows a clear ambivalence of the state towards a complete overhaul; instead, it retained much of traditional Hindu law relating to the family, while attempting to introduce change on an issue of fundamental significance within traditional Hindu law. The public/private dichotomy is a self-perpetuating one. There is a dialectical link between the ideology of the 'private' and the non-recognition and undervaluation of women's work by the state and law. Where the law constructs the 'private' and places women firmly within it, so also it emerges that wherever women are becomes the 'private' in relation to law and the state. So, for example, the fact of women working in agriculture is not recognized and is rendered insignificant, by virtue of the fact that 'it is for the family' or 'pin money', making it a 'private' activity and therefore outside the scope of consideration.

These issues within the liberal tradition, which are challenged by feminists also bear upon the significant problem of the difficulty in securing substantive rights as opposed to formal rights. In its universal, abstract, individual subject liberalism ignores the realities of the individual, and all her attendant characteristics. Gender, class, status, power, age, religion or caste in the context of India are obscured or ignored. As Pathak and Rajan have summarized, taking the state's treatment of the subject in the controversial Shah Bano Case:[7]

> Certainly, the Constitution of India, following Western constitutional models, did envisage (this) unity of the Indian subject within the legal system …. In the ideal, subjects in law are undifferentiated, non-descript, equal and singular (Pathak and Rajan, 1989, 573–577).

Thus, where the impetus for addressing gender inequalities seems to be derived from an agenda of law reform in India, it is even more problematic (Menon, 1995; Kapur and Cossman, 1996). Where women are simply 'brought within' legal provisions, without sufficiently taking account of their realities in terms of religion, caste or class, the gap law reform seeks to bridge will continue.

'Modernity' in Indian Law and Its Engagement with the Past

The liberal, democratic constitutional framework characterizing the independent Indian state is tied to the particular historical processes involved in and leading up to the formation of the independent state. Modernity was a core principle or aim around which the debates within the reform movement were organized, as well as within the nationalist movement. The Constitutional and legal framework of post-independent India is imbued with this. In particular, the rationale of most 'progressive' legislation in post-independent India has been the explicit adherence to 'modern' 'civilised' notions of the status of individuals and the role of the state towards securing these.

For example, addressing the question of who demanded changes to the HSA, the Hindu Law Committee expressed the following:

---

7   *Mohammed Ahmed Khan v Shah Bano Khan* AIR 1985 SC 945.

... but more important than any other happenings in India are the repercussion of the events in the international sphere ... India has been participating in international conferences and pleadings for human rights ... with an eloquence which has commanded universal admiration. The eyes of the world are upon her now and it would be more than a misfortune if at this juncture she were to fail to enact ... a Hindu code in which there was equality before the law and in which disabilities based on caste or sex were no longer recognised. We are now almost bound in honour to remove these .... This should be a sufficient answer to the question as to, who demands these changes in law? (Report of the Hindu Law Committee, 1947, 5).

The adoption of a new Constitution in independent India with the simultaneous retention of the legal, judicial and administrative framework reflects post-colonial India's continuing engagement with the past, colonial processes. One significant aspect of this continuance is the principle of modernity, which itself was a product of colonial discourse (Kidder, 1978). The concept of modern as opposed to the traditional was at the heart of the various debates preceding independence. The social reform debates, the impact of European scholarship on India and British administrative policy gave impetus to the 'modernisation' of India. At the same time, the orthodox opposition to reform and the impact of orientalism argued for the perfection of 'Indian tradition' to be maintained.

These opposing movements were however organized around the same principle, that of religious sanction. Therefore, while the reformists sought to argue that the 'modern' was indeed in keeping with the true spirit of the Hindu religion, therefore sanctioned by it, the orthodoxy used their interpretation of religion to argue that it did not sanction the changes sought. British administrative policy and official discourse formed the basis upon which religion became the legitimizing principle (Derrett, 1968).[8] Critiques have also come from scholars looking at the construction of issues and debates within colonial engagement. In particular, the implementation of law and its reform proved to be a predominant arena for these debates, and as such, law provided the basis for the embodiment of the outcomes within it. Lata Mani provides a vivid account of this process in the context of Sati, where time and again court pundits were referred the question 'whether the practice was sanctioned by religious texts' (Mani, 1990, 100). The same is to be seen, for example, in the case of courtesans (Oldenberg 1990; Nair, 1993) and in the debates surrounding the issues of widow remarriage and age of consent (Chakravarti, 1990, 1998; Chaudhury, 1990, 1993).

The reform movement was a significant part of the debates preceding the nationalist movement and independence. Western education and its ideas of humanitarianism, rationalism and liberalism provided the basis for questioning accepted practices within Hindu society, and utilitarian ideas were the new framework for evaluating these (Desai, 1959; Natarajan, 1959). What is of particular significance for our purposes, however, in the interplay of reformist agendas and the privileging of religion within the structure of the discourse, is that women were pre-eminent signifiers of the issues, both constructed and addressed by the debate as

---

8   For a more formal historical account of the British administration in India, see Basu, 1983; Gledhill, 1964; Jain (1966).

the embodiment of 'tradition' (Mazumdar, 1976; Nanda, 1976; Chakravarti, 1990; Sangari and Vaid, 1990; Chatterjee, 1993; Chhachhi, 1994). This problem has been aptly brought out by the remark of Uma Chakravarti:

> The entangled relationship between law, custom, caste, property and gender was not so easy to disentangle ... (Chakravarti, 1998, 134).

The subsequent nationalist movement was itself founded upon the principles set up earlier (Desai, 1959; Heimsath, 1964). The means to create a new national identity was based upon the fundamental premise that had been in operation in the previous debates: the essential difference between the colonial masters and the subjects was based upon tradition. Nationalist thought (as a derivative of colonial thought), argued that while modern European culture possesses attributes that enable its people towards power and progress, these attributes are missing in the 'traditional' societies under domination (Said, 1978; Chatterjee, 1993). Further, it argues that such domination is not unchangeable, for the cultural attributes are not immutable and modernity defines the change that is sought, for nationalism:

> ... asserts that the superiority of the West lies in the materialism of its culture, exemplified by its science, technology and love of progress, But the East is superior in the spiritual aspect of culture .... *True modernity* of the non-European nations would lie in combining the superior material qualities of the West with the spiritual greatness of the East ... (Chatterjee, 1993, 51; emphasis added).

The story so far, of the history of nationalism and debates preceding it, illustrates the key role of 'modernity' and 'tradition' as opposing concepts in the search towards what could characterize the 'Indian', which could be the basis for forging a new national identity through independence. This is indeed the basis upon which the modern, liberal post colonial state was formed, and which is implicit in the contemporary constitutional and legal framework. Although it was the elite who could be identified with this modernizing spirit of the nationalist movement, it is relevant to note that the policy makers under Nehru in post-independent India were these very same elites (Rai, 1999).

The continued engagement of the post-colonial state with the debates of the past is evident in the framework adopted by the state itself. While independence brought the adoption of a new Constitution, a vast body of judicial and administrative law continued as before with minor changes. The Constitution explicitly provides for the continuance of laws passed before its inception subject to certain conditions.[9] Moreover, this engagement continues to privilege religion and the concept of 'tradition'. Thus, the very constitution of 'Hindu law' in legislation and its implementation by the judiciary continues to be structured upon the same principles as in the processes prior to independence (Smith, 1963). This has significant implications upon the constructions and definitions of a 'Hindu woman', her role and identity. The attempt to 'modernise' her status through legislative reform in the

---

9 Article 13, Constitution of India, 1950.

post-colonial state is in fact constituted by this engagement, and ultimately fails to overcome it, thereby losing to a great extent its transformative potential.

Further, this continued construction of Hindu women within the framework of religious and traditional social structures, combined with the liberal distinction between the private/public, results in the state and law ignoring the material context within which women also live. By constructing women and their interests solely within the context of the social and religious structures, the law defines these only in terms of the family as the unit of society. Religion and tradition (and derived ideology) are constructed as the only operative forces in women's lives. This results in the exclusion of the factors of class and gender, among others, as they affect women's lives even within the family. By providing rules in respect to succession to family property, and women's right to this, Hindu law may be seen to be going beyond the limitations of liberalism in addressing women within the family and bringing it within the scope of law. However, by privileging religion and excluding a significant aspect of women's lives within the 'family' as peasants engaged in production, Hindu law actually limits its own conception of women. Thus, while it may seem that Hindu law in fact breaks down law's reluctance to enter the domain of the 'private' sphere of women's lives by touching upon the family, the parameters within which this is done, combined with its non-recognition of the material aspect of women's 'private' lives in the domain of work and production in effect, serves to reinforce the exclusion of women's interests from law (Parasher, 1997).

The discussion highlights that the particular construction of women's claim to land, as 'Hindu' women's right to family land through succession, is in fact a derivative of the broader constitutional framework. This discussion brings out the limitations of a liberal constitutional approach to law as a means of bringing about social change, which, as has been noted, has dominated the engagement with law reform in India. The discussion further brings out the particular issue of women's claim to independent land ownership, that their interest is limited within law's construction of the claim within this framework.

Legal Pluralism

The multi-cultural and multi-religious context of Indian society requires a discussion of legal pluralism. The existence of plural bodies of law applicable to persons according to their religion is in itself a reflection of legal pluralism. Further, the colonial history of India has resulted in many instances and aspects of law instituted during the colonial regime continuing in post-independence India. The incorporation of common law within the Indian legal system as a result of British legal policy is an example of this.

Theories of legal pluralism have been advanced in a number of contexts. The study of customary law in 'indigenous' societies through the process of colonialism has provided rich understandings of people's interaction with plural legal orders (Chanock, 1985; Merry, 1988). This work has been further developed by research in Southern and Eastern Africa and the development of 'women's law', which has engaged a deep analysis of women's location within a variety of norms and structures (Bentzon et al., 1998). The work of Scandinavian scholars has further developed analysis of norms within the administrative centres, and at other locales outside state law in the context of the Scandinavian countries.

Falk Moore (1978) has developed the concept of the 'semi-autonomous social field', arguing that:

> between the body politic and the individual, there are interposed various smaller organised social fields to which the individual 'belongs'. These social fields have their own customs and rules and means of coercion or inducing compliance (Moore, 1978, 58).

Although Bentzon et al. point to a difference between 'anthropologists' legal pluralism' and lawyers' legal pluralism, arguing that the 'semi-autonomous social field', as developed by Moore (1978), is a descriptive rather than normative concept (Bentzon et al., 1998), it is useful precisely for enabling the recognition and description of the many structures and norms that affect women. As Petersen has argued:

> Including sub-state levels of normative systems and structures as a subject of study is both relevant and crucial if the aim is to increase knowledge of the actual legal situation of women in most countries. Such knowledge is necessary to put forward appropriate, relevant and realistic demands for changes in order to bring about actual improvements in the lives of women (Petersen, 1997, 152).

Legal pluralism furthers our analysis of women's claim to land ownership as established by law in a number of ways. Firstly, it allows an analysis of the normative role of religion in women's lives. As we have discussed, law constructs women's claim to land on the basis of religious ideology and defines it as a right to 'Hindu' women, located within the family. Although it may be said that state law is in fact recognizing 'Hindu' principles and incorporating them within it, legal pluralism provides the basis upon which the contours of the normative effect of 'Hindu' law may be examined, and not merely assumed. It enables us to explore the extent to which 'Hindu' law 'exist as social fact because it receives social observance' (Woodman, 1997, 183).

Secondly, the meaning of legal pluralism derives from its recognition that there are regulatory or normative systems other than formal law that affect and control people's lives. In studying women's lives as they are affected by law, in particular, scholars have argued for the adoption of a broader approach (Dahl, 1986; Petersen, 1997; Bentzon et al., 1998). In order to describe, understand and improve the position of women in society, Dahl emphasizes empirical data about the lived realities of women in society. The operation of legal rules and the sources of law and legal doctrine are fundamental sources to analyse the complex interrelationship between law and life as they affect women (Dahl in Bentzon et al., 1998). This, it is argued, means that:

> In addition to conventional legal sources such as case law, statutes, subsidiary legislation, legal theories in textbooks and articles, the practices in fora where the arrangements which directly affect the position of women are made, are also examined. Examples of such fora are the family, the workplace, the church community, the local courts and administrative agencies (Bentzon et al., 1998, 66–67).

This perspective obtains a wider scope for the consideration of law, for law is seen as a rule generating and rule upholding process that takes place in various locales (Bentzon et al., 1998). A recognition of the plural and non-hierarchical structure of norms that affect women's lives leads to an

> ... understanding of legal norms − or legal sources − as being engendered by different, overlapping, coexisting, co-operating and/or competing structures ... a more profound examination and evaluation of both diverse types of norms and of the different values underlying such different normative systems ... (Petersen, 1997, 154).

This understanding allows the analysis of norms that operate upon women's lives in a variety of contexts. Thus, in the analysis of rural women's claim to land in India, legal pluralism allows for the consideration of the statutory norms under the HSA, the operation of Hindu religious norms upon women and the evaluation of norms by which they are affected as workers in agriculture. Legal pluralism allows, in addition, to evaluate the operation of norms within the family, the wider society, the household, and the farm. As Petersen strongly argues:

> To my view it implies that both norms generated in families, workplaces, tribes, social and religious communities must be studied, considered and addressed in their complex interrelation if an improvement in the situation of women is to be achieved, and if the contribution of women to society can be acknowledged, valued and taken general advantage of for the benefit of both men and women, old and young (Petersen, 1997, 157).

Thirdly, therefore, legal pluralism provides the basis upon which the interaction between the various normative structures may be evaluated. In the case of evaluating Hindu women's claim to land, it would allow for an analysis of the impact of religious norms upon the statutory norms and vice versa. It would also enable the interrelation between the norms affecting women's role in agriculture and the religious and statutory norms. Hindu women in their relation to land ownership, are governed by a combination of legal, social and cultural norms, values and institutions. To study the role and impact or effectiveness of one of these, namely statutory norms, is to overlook the essential interlinkages and impact of the others. It follows also, that to embark upon a process of increasing gendered access to resources through law, an understanding of the ways in which it may do so is essential. This not only prevents the exclusive emphasis on statutory law, based upon an erroneous assumption of its overriding power, but it also allows for more informed methods to be adopted. Methods that are informed upon the precise interdependence and interconnectedness of cultural values, religious norms, gender ideology and social organization, in order to evaluate the maximum effectiveness of the statutory norm.

Legal pluralism addresses the critique of liberalism by providing the basis for law to shift its focus from the public world where it has hitherto been, to those arenas which are significant in their regulation of individuals. For a vast majority of women in the world, particularly in developing countries, this is the family/household. This is where they carry out their daily activities and by extension where they are most regulated. The issue of inheritance derives directly from the Hindu notion of 'family', as the property in question does not disturb distinctions made in Hindu law between ancestral and personal property. The effect of this is to strengthen and continue the operation of the family, specifically the coparcenary, of which is the ancestral property. Thus, the gender ideology operative here is directly derived from norms and notions related to the 'family'.

It therefore provides, within legal analysis, the means to make the links between women as 'Hindu' women subject to norms of the family and religious ideology, and women as peasants, affected by norms in relation to work and production in agriculture. In conjunction, it allows for the focus of legal analysis into domains that it does not enter, and upon norms that the law does not recognize. Taken together, it provides within legal analysis the conceptual 'bridge' between the two aspects of the dichotomy posed earlier. Therefore, legal pluralism is a further critique of liberal law's restricted gaze and law's exclusion from 'private' domains such as the family within liberalism. It provides the analytical tool for moving towards a broader conceptualization of gendered perspectives within law, to generate a better understanding of women's lives as they are affected by law in a variety of contexts.

Contextualizing Law: Taking Account of Women's Lives

This section elaborates upon a central theme that has emerged within legal pluralism, particularly as it has been used to investigate and develop 'women's law' by scholars in the Southern and East African and Scandinavian contexts (Dahl, 1986; Petersen, 1992, 1997; Bentzon et al., 1998). This development emphasizes the need to develop analyses of law in order to explain and improve women's lives, and argues that the principal means by which this may be achieved is by taking into account women's 'lived realities' as they affect their interaction with law.

In 'Towards a sociology of Indian law', the call was made by Baxi 20 years ago that 'a rational comprehension of the role of legal systems in social stability and growth demands a more wide-ranging awareness of law as a social system' (Baxi, 1986, 3). At the risk of being accused of making gross generalizations, I believe it would be true to say that the impact of law as a normative system in people's everyday lives is minimal in Indian society. This is not to say that the *belief* in law as a relevant means to address these is diminished, but that the *perceived* gap in law's supposed power and actual ability to influence people's lives is wide (Gandhi and Shah, 1992). The most casual study must acknowledge this gap, and even upon a very preliminary analysis one is faced with a range of factors that are obviously significant in accounting for this gap. At the most basic level, poverty, illiteracy, language barriers, and insurmountable distances are only some that operate to limit access to the most 'real' or 'visible' aspect of law: the courts (Dhagamwar, 1992). In this sense at least, the most cursory student of law in India must take into account the impact of these social realities upon law. Any further study of law in terms of this perceived gap, which is itself based upon expectations of law to provide solutions, must therefore acknowledge the social context within which operates. If one acknowledges the relevance of Baxi's statement that '... understanding of lawyers' law (that is legal processes as relevant to decision makers or lawmen – judges, lawyers, law reformers and jurists) is almost impossible without a sensitive grasp of the implications of law as a social process' law (Baxi, 1986, 1), it is even more so in the study of Indian law.

At the heart of this study is the conviction that in order to understand the legal position of the women, it is necessary to focus upon the lives of the women as they are actually lived. The conception of a 'legal position' is based upon an abstraction; upon the organization and analysis of ideas and concepts within an epistemological frame that gives meaning to and justifies or validates our ideas and concepts. In order to fully understand the way in which these abstractions become operationalized and constitute an aspect of reality, it is necessary to deal with the everyday lives of the women who make it so. Similarly, if we wish to understand the phenomenon where the abstractions remain, and has not become operationalized, one must again focus on the lives of the women as they are lived and experienced, in order to do so. The relation of the women's legal position must be explored through the facts and experiences that constitute their lives.

Therefore, women's daily experiences must generate the 'problem' requiring exploration. While Smith is concerned mainly with sociology when she says that this 'provides the starting point for a more adequate sociology' (Smith, 1987, 84), the principle remains true for legal analysis. Women's relationship, if any, to inheritance rights must begin to be understood with the problems that their lives might present within the context of inheritance. Again, to reverse the position, we can best begin with an exploration of the women's lives in relation to the land within their particular context in order to understand and analyse one specific aspect of that relation, namely ownership through inheritance.

What therefore is the identity of the women in the Hindu small peasant household within their familial and social context? Does this identity form the premise upon which a particular relationship to land ownership is constructed? Does it operate to define and maintain notions of legitimacy of women's right to ownership? How is their work contribution perceived by the women, and how does this, if at all, relate to the construction of their identity? Is the notion of legitimacy, constructed by socio-cultural context, affected by evaluations of work contribution?

Using the perspective of the women's experience to generate the problematic, and by using the experiences as the reality against which hypothesis are tested (Harding, 1987, 7) leads to a more complete understanding of any given aspect of social relation. The conception of law must be understood in its historical and contextual perspective.

To the extent that law must be made to take cognizance of, and account for, continued substantive inequality, a fuller understanding and analysis of the specificities that constitute women's 'lived realities', encompassing both the material as well as the ideological, would allow insights into the particularities of law as it may make a substantive impact upon women's lived experiences.

Taking account of the 'totality' of women's lives establishes the basis upon which we can extend our analysis of women's location and experience as peasants within family households. In addition to a consideration of their lives as they are structured by religion within the family, analysis of Hindu women's role as peasants and workers and contributors to agricultural production is complementary to broadening the scope of the analysis.

Perspectives on Work and Contributions

Thus far, I have discussed the framework with which law may be seen to construct women's claim to land primarily on the basis of religion and located within the family. Legal pluralism presents us with an understanding that is closest to extending law's construction to include women as peasants, located within the household, engaged in work and production. Within this, the arguments for contextualizing law to take women's 'lived realities' into account provide a means for operationalizing such extended analyses. This section discusses the particular aspect of woman's work and contributions as significant to my analysis of woman's 'lived realities'. It is argued that in the case of rural peasant women in India, perspectives on their work and contributions are crucial to evaluating the particular context of their lives. Taking account of women's work and contributions in peasant households in India leads us to explore the context of women as peasants, within households, engaged in work and production in agriculture, in addition to an analysis which addresses them as Hindu women within the family, affected by religious ideology.

In examining the role of law in entitling women to land ownership within rural Indian society, an examination of women's work becomes significant for two reasons. First, a vast majority of the law's 'subjects', the Hindu women in rural households, are in fact 'workers' in those households. Moreover, it is the absence of ownership of land that determines their position as such, for without land they remain 'workers'. This therefore constitutes a very significant aspect of the reality that law must acknowledge and consider. Secondly, if policies (including law) are to adequately address gendered access to resources they must acknowledge women's role in production (Beneria, 1988). Beneria has argued that women's work needs to be reconceptualized and assigned its relative value in order that 'women's role in society may be placed in its proper perspective' (Beneria, 1988, 373). Where ideological assumptions are the basis for regarding women's work as secondary and subordinate to men's, this is reinforced by the lack of a clear conceptualization of women's role in economic activity (Ginwala et al., 1990). Addressing the issue of whether it would be useful for women to move beyond conventional concepts of the labour force and include women's role, Beneria identifies three main objectives for such an exercise:

> ... (1) to counteract the ideological undervaluation of women's work and give recognition to the long hours of labour in which they are involved ... (2) the need to have as much information as possible about women's activities and their role in economic life. Planning development programmes ... must be based on accurate information if they are to be fully relevant to about 50 per cent of the world's population ... (3) to define economic activity in such a way as to relate it to human welfare ... (Beneria, 1988, 384–385).

Thus, in addressing the issue of increased access to land for rural women, a fuller analysis of the framework of law must incorporate these issues. In order to incorporate women's role in production within our analysis we must first address the ideological construction of women's work, while also addressing the conceptual basis upon which women's work is defined. In the context of Hindu peasant women in small farming households, therefore, the cultural values forming the basis of gender ideology, and the material reality of their role and contribution in agriculture need to be analysed in order to explore the dialectical links between the two. The effectiveness of property rights for these women may thereafter be seen in terms of the relationship of the legal structures to the existing dialectical links between gender ideology and material reality. Does the legal system strengthen and reinforce these links, or break them? Does it take account of these existing links and thereafter provide a structural basis for change?

Recent analyses of women's work in agriculture in India has repeatedly brought out the centrality of the need to consider the issue of women's work within the cultural context in which particular gender issues are defined (Bardhan, 1985; Sharma, 1985; Ahmed-Ghosh, 1993; Mencher, 1993). Gender relations in India continue to be defined by the ideology of gender, class and caste ideology which is the product of the dominant patriarchal ideology. As The World Bank report on Gender and Poverty in India (1991) states, the pervasive gender ideology affects the type of work women seek and are considered suitable for. The need to comprehensively analyse women's role in production, particularly in developing societies within an agricultural base has led to extending the analysis of women's work within the household. The invisibility of women's work has been exposed, primarily by the inclusion of house work and work within the household as 'work' (Sharma, 1985; Papanek, 1989; Bagchi and Raju, 1993).

In other words, the analysis of women's role in production, can be possible in such societies only by uncovering the 'purdah' (veil) that shrouds women's work; by looking 'inside' the domain that is predominantly female, and the range of tasks that are accomplished by women within the domain, the household (Ginwala et al., 1990). Once this is achieved, women's actual role and contribution, particularly to agricultural production, can begin to be estimated.[10] In the Indian context, those engaged in the analysis of women's work are arguing for the inclusion of the time spent on the food, fuel and water collection as 'work', and have started to question the classical market orientated definition of 'work' (Bagchi and Raju, 1993). Looking at women's reality and position in relation to law entails an understanding of the structures and their relations within these that result in their position. Within the specific context of inheritance to agricultural land in an Indian village, therefore, this would mean to include an understanding of her relation to the land as a worker/producer; her ability to own appropriate/own it as a beneficiary; and the processes and meanings whereby these are instituted and maintained, and which thereafter establish the basis of her interaction or non-interaction with the law, or non-engagement with the law.

---

10   Where there is a continuum of activities ranging from the house work proper/domestic tasks to support task within the household such as preparing meals for the workers, or taking food to the workers in the field, the question remains – where should the line be drawn so as to calculate the 'women's work'? Should such a line be drawn?

Gender and Access to Resources

The effort to explore and analyse the factors affecting Hindu women within small peasant households in their ability to own land requires us to address the relation between gender and access to resources, and to analyse, in particular, the way in which gender affects or impacts upon access to resources. Since the inception of various strategies to address women's place within economic development, the issue of increasing gendered access to resources has been a significant part of efforts at mainstreaming gender within development policies (Tinker, 1990; Weiringa, 1994; Kabeer, 1995; Vishwanathan et al., 1997). Subsequently, within the broader literature on gender and development, more and more has come to be written of women's roles in economic development (Boserup, 1970; Beneria and Sen, 1997): the extent and nature of women's contribution to economic development; the embeddedness of social, political and cultural relations within economic ones, and the need to consider all in addressing gendered effects (Elson, 1991; Moser, 1993); the need to address and account for women's work (Bardhan, 1985; Dixon-Mueller, 1985; Beneria, 1988) and various specific studies detailing women's work in various contexts.

These are some of the areas developed by those working on issues relating to gender and development. The fundamental notions have not everywhere been understood to mean the same. Rather there is severe contestation and discussion over issues of what constitutes 'development' (Adelman and Paliwala, 1993; Stewart, 1993; Sen, 1999; Rai, 2002); how is gender to be characterized; what constitute specific gender interests, the addressing of which would therefore lead to 'empowerment' (Weiringa, 1994; Kabeer, 1995; Gasper, 1996; Charlton, 1997; Molyneux, 1998; Hill, 2003); who defines these and who/what do they represent (Chowdhry, 1995; Hirshman, 1996); and what are understood to be the conditions of those who are to 'benefit' from such 'development' (Mukhopadhyay, 1985; Mazumdar and Sharma, 1990; Ranadive, 1994; Harcourt, 1997; Gasper and Staveren, 2003). These are but a few of the issues that have been debated.

The focus generated by debates over development and the particular importance of addressing the gender dimensions of participation and benefits from development policies has also contributed to explorations of the ways in which access and participation are determined by gender. It has been established that gender determines to a significant extent and manner in which access to resources becomes available, as well as the means by which such access may be defined or legitimized. Whereas the notions of 'need' and 'rights' are primarily accepted as the basis of resource allocation and distribution, many have argued that the very definition of these notions are tied to the issue of gender (Ferguson, 1988; Jonasdottir, 1988; Fraser, 1989; Moore, 1995).

Gender identities, as they constitute gender relations (Moore, 1995) determine the rights and needs of particular individuals that are established. This requires a process of contestation whereby a need becomes established as a right, where not only the satisfaction of needs are contested, but also the definition and interpretation of the same. To quote Fraser:

I take the politics of need to comprise three moments that are analytically distinct but inter-related in practise. The first is the struggle to establish or deny the political status of a given need, the struggle to validate the need as a matter of legitimate political concern or to enclose it as a non-political matter. The second is the struggle over the interpretation of the need, the struggle for the power to define it, and so, to determine what would satisfy it. The third moment is the struggle over the satisfaction of the need, the struggle to secure or withhold provision (Fraser, 1989, 163).

In relation to women and land, the contestation is at all these three levels: to establish the need for women's right in land, to define the parameters of that need, and to translate that need into actual rights in practice. Therefore, in order to understand women's access to land as a resource, it is essential to conceptualize it within the framework of the social relations that determine gender relations and which in turn affect property relations. Gender relations refers to the relations of power between women and men which are revealed in a range of practices, ideas and representations, including the division of labour, roles and resources between women and men, and the ascribing to them of different abilities, attitudes, desires, personality traits, behavioural patterns and so on (Moore, 1995). Taken as largely socially constructed rather than biologically determined, gender relations are both constituted by and help constitute these practices and ideologies in interaction with other structures of social hierarchy such as caste, class and race.

Agarwal echoes this in arguing for the recognition of the dialectical link between the material context and the gender ideology in conceptualizing gender and access to property (Agarwal, 1995). She argues that establishing gendered access to resources requires contestation over matters which are simultaneously material and ideological, acting with and reinforcing one another, where gender ideologies can obstruct women from obtaining property rights. Ideas about gender underlie practices such as female seclusion, which erode women's personal autonomy through the control of women's mobility and sexual freedom (Dyson and Moore, 1983; Gandhi and Shah, 1992; Bagwe, 1995). These ideologies and associated practices restrict both women's ability to exercise their existing property claims and to successfully challenge persisting gender inequalities in law, public policy and practice in relation to their claims (Dyson and Moore, 1983; Agarwal, 1994).

The link between gender relations, as an aspect of social relations, and property brings into focus the need to locate explorations of gendered access to property within the cultural and social systems within which they operate, for

... property is not primarily a relation between people and things, but a relation between people and people − a social relation or a set of social relations (Whitehead, 1984, 176).

The need to look at kinship relations within which property, marriage and labour are embedded, and which control women's control over property, is brought out extensively in Sharma's work (Sharma, 1989). She discusses women, work and property in North West India and concludes that there is a very real difference in women's and men's relationship to property, highlighted by the fact that very few women exercise their rights under the Hindu Succession Act, 1956 (Sharma, 1989).[11] Whitehead suggests that since concepts of property are ultimately bound up with the concepts of the person we need to look at how kinship systems help to construct men and women in different ways, as different sorts of persons (Whitehead, 1984). In her view, it is the kinship family system which constructs women in such a way that they are less able to act as fully operative subjects. She notes that

> A woman's capacity to "own" things depends on the extent to which she is legally and actually separable from other people, the issue raised is the extent to which forms of conjugal familial and kinship allow her a individual existence so that she can assert rights as an individual against individuals (Whitehead, 1984, 189).

The issue raised is the extent to which forms of conjugal, familial and kinship relations allow her an independent existence so that she can assert her rights as an individual. Conjugal, familial and kinship systems appear often to operate so as to construct the position of women as subordinate, such that by carrying kinship (or familial or conjugal) status women are less free to act as full subjects in relation to things and people (Whitehead, 1984).

Although as Moore (1991) points out, this echoes the idea of the 'domestic' as enforcing powerlessness, and the family as the site of women's oppression, it brings out the need to extend the analysis of the law to relations and organizations, and locate it beyond the public spheres into the household. The role of kinship, family and the household structures as they operate towards constructing women's identity must be addressed. Further, the way in which particular gendered relations of production and distribution within these structures establish norms for legitimacy must be analysed. This would provide the basis for an understanding of how these identities are linked to access to property within the legal framework.

The Bargaining Approach

This analysis of Hindu women's traditional and continued exclusion from property develops upon the specific location of women within the particular structures of the family and (membership of a religious) community on the one hand and the household and wider economy on the other. Where women may be conceptualized as located within the family, a gendered analysis of access to property can draw upon the bargaining approach as developed by Sen and Agarwal (Sen, 1983, 1985, 1987; Agarwal, 1997, 1994). Land may be identified, within this approach, as a resource accessed by the members of the family through negotiation. The outcome of the negotiation for the members involved would be determined by their respective fallback positions, where the outcome would be favourable if, failing a co-operative solution, a person would be in no worse position than before.

---

11 Sharma also gives an insightful analysis on the significance (or not) of dowry as a form of property that has traditionally been accorded to women in Indian society. As she puts it, 'dowry goes *with* the daughter *to* the son-in-law', thereby refuting the claim that dowry may be considered women's property (Sharma, 1989, 163).

Amartya Sen's analysis of the bargaining model introduces further dimensions (Sen, 1983, 1985, 1987). He recognizes that the outcome of bargaining will depend not only on a person's fall-back position should co-operation cease, but also on what he terms 'perceived interest response' and 'perceived contribution response'. The outcome will be less favourable to a person: (a) the less value s/he attaches to her/his own well being relative to the well being of others (perceived interest response), and (b) the smaller her/his contribution to the household is *perceived* to *be* (perceived contribution response).

Discussing the role of perceptions and disputing the identification of well-being with the fulfilment of perceived interests, Sen (1987) makes room for the causal influence of perceptions on ideas of propriety and legitimacy of different institutional arrangements and through that on the respective well-beings of men and women. He argues that perceptions of legitimacy and desert must be included in the analysis, since the assumption of clear and unambiguous perceptions of individual interests within the bargaining approach misses crucial aspects of the nature of gender divisions within and outside the family. The sense of appropriateness is related to ambiguities of perception of interests, and with certain perceived notions of legitimacy regarding what is 'deserved' and what is not, and the specification of felt individual interests must recognize perception problems.

Understanding of interests, well-being, obligations, objectives and legitimate behaviour is influenced by diverse identities and in some contexts the family identity may exert such a strong influence on perceptions that formulation of any clear notion of individual welfare may be difficult. In the context of traditional societies such as India, for example, family-centred perceptions may be so strong that,

> … if a typical Indian woman were asked about her personal "welfare" she would find the
> question unintelligible, and if she is able to reply, she may answer the question in terms of
> her reading of the welfare of her family … (Sen, 1987, 7).

Sen and Kynch (1983) note that various patterns of systemic discrimination may well be built into the sense of propriety as to who should get what (for example, it could be that it is regarded as unquestionably 'right' that the head of the family should get the largest share of the food when it is in short supply). Rural family members in South Asian countries like India may not have any clear perception of individual welfare, having instead some unsplittable notion of family well-being. That notion of family well-being may not be at all of the neutral, individualist type, and may incorporate systemic biases in favour of fulfilling the needs of some family members, for example males. Further, even the *perception* of the relative needs of different family members may be closely related to a sense of *priorities*, for example there may be the magnification of the needs of the males in general and the head of the household in particular (Sen and Kynch, 1983, 364).

They illustrate the point with an example of perception bias in a post-famine health survey in India. In Singur, near Calcutta, in 1944 − the year after the Bengal Famine of 1943 − the All India Institute of Hygiene and Public Health carried out a health survey which included questions about the perception of one's own health. There were many widows and widowers in the population surveyed. In reply to the question as to whether they were 'ill' or of 'indifferent' health, 48.5 per cent of the widowers confided to being thus afflicted, while the corresponding number of widows was merely 2.5 per cent. The contrast is even more interesting when we look at the response to the question as to whether one was in 'indifferent' health, leaving out the category of being 'ill', for which some clear-cut medical criteria do exist. 45.6 % of the widowers confessed to having the perception of being indifferent in health. In contrast, the proportion of widows who had that perception was – it is reported – exactly zero! (Sen and Kynch, 1983, 364).

In focusing on perceptions, we are able to distinguish between well being and personal welfare, where the lack of personal interest combined with a great concern for family welfare is just the kind of attitude that helps to sustain traditional inequalities in intra-family divisions of resources.[12] Further, personal interest and welfare are not just matters of perception. There are objective aspects to it such as the person's functioning and capabilities: what she is able to do or be, for example, the ability to be well-nourished, to read and write, to take part in community life or to appear in public without shame (Sen, 1985, 1987).

The following are the factors, identified by Sen, which would determine the outcome of bargaining and negotiation for the individual concerned, as developed by the bargaining approach. The outcome of bargaining and negotiation may be seen to be the result of these.

Breakdown Well-Being Response[13]

This refers to the position from which a person enters into the bargaining process as it affects the outcome. A particular solution is arrived at because if a person were to be in a worse position in the event of the bargaining process breaking down, than within the solution arrived at, any other solution arrived at through negotiation would be less favourable to her.

The breakdown position gives the person vulnerability or strength in bargaining. If, in the case of a breakdown, one of the persons is going to end up in greater difficulty than previously, it weakens that person's ability to secure a favourable outcome. Where, for example, women come to believe that no other option is available, the situation of dependence upon the family for support and survival may be understood in terms of their worsened well-being should the existing outcome of the bargaining change. In other words, the weakness of their fall-back position is reflected in their position of overwhelming dependence. Factors such as greater illiteracy, persistent childbearing, norms of social exclusion and invisibility, loss

---

12 As Sen puts it, the underdog may come to accept the legitimacy of the unequal order and become an implicit accomplice, and 'it can be a serious error to take the absence of protests and questioning of inequality as evidence of the absence of that inequality' (Sen, 1987, 8).

13 'Given other things, if the breakdown position of one were worse in terms of well-being, then the collusive solution, if different, would be less favourable to her well-being' (Sen, 1987, 22).

of honour and status, among others, can lead to a weak breakdown position of women in particular within societies such as India.

Perceived Interest Response[14]

According to this, the solution arrived at would be affected by perceptions of self-interest towards a person's own well-being. Where the perception of self-interest attaches less value to her well-being, the outcome would be less favourable to such person, in terms of her well-being.

Sen argues that the influence of perceived interest on measures of well-being may be that the outcome may be formed by choosing a solution not on the basis of individual well-being, but that of perceived interests (Sen, 1987). The person may get a worse deal in the collusive solution if her perceived interest takes little note of her own well being, as in cases where there is a bias against her individual interest.

Agarwal departs from this, debating his conceptualization of 'perceived interest response' and its importance in determining the outcomes of bargaining in terms of women's welfare, disagreeing that women tend to have a less sharp perception of their individual interests in societies like India. She argues that to the extent that women do seek to maximize 'family' welfare, this could still be consistent with their long-term self-interest (even if it is at the cost of their immediate well-being), *in so far as women are more dependent on the family for their survival than men, both economically and socially*. Further, women may sacrifice their individual interests for the interests of family members out of conscious choice, but the notion of family itself needs probing. Sacrificing for one's children may well reduce a woman's well-being, but this need not be a case of false perception on her part, as both altruism and the pursuit of self-interest can be self-aware actions (Agarwal, 1997, 1994).

She also debates Sen's understanding that they may suffer from a form of 'false consciousness' about their own well being. Noting that the empirical evidence on this is limited, and that which exists suggests women's overt compliance with practices which disadvantage them, she argues that this does not necessarily mean that they accept those practices as legitimate. On the contrary, she argues, their perceptions are better revealed in their many covert forms of resistance to gender inequities (Agarwal, 1997, 1994).

Perceived Contribution Response[15]

Here consideration is given to the contribution a person is perceived to be making towards the overall wealth of the group within which negotiations are being carried

---

14 'Given other things, if the self-interest perception of one of the persons were to attach less value to her own well-being, then the collusive solution, if different, be less favourable to that person, in terms of well-being' (Sen, 1987, 23).

15 'Given other things, if in the accounting of respective outcomes, a person were perceived as making a larger contribution to the overall opulence of the group, then the

out. Where a person is perceived to make a greater contribution to the overall wealth of the group, the outcome would be more favourable to that person.

Here, *perceived* contributions have to be distinguished from *actual* contributions. The perceived contribution of people can directly affect the 'legitimacy' of enjoying the corresponding share of the fruits of co-operation. The nature of perceived contribution also has to be distinguished from the amount of time spent in working inside and outside the home. For example, time allocation studies show that women seem to do large amounts of work even when the so-called 'economic' contribution is perceived to be relatively modest (Mencher, 1994).

Sen places considerable importance on a woman's earnings outside the home for giving her a stronger fall-back position, and a clearer perception of her own well-being, and a higher valuation of her contribution (Sen, 1987). Agarwal makes the argument that the notion of legitimacy needs to be broader than that that captured by Sen's 'perceived contribution response'. Notions of legitimate shares may stem from a variety of ethical principles, of which a person's contribution is only one, and the principle of need may be another. Reducing the gap between women's actual contributions and social perceptions about their contributions may not, on their own, strengthen the legitimacy of their claims and improve their consumption shares (as Sen suggests), if, for instance, the criterion for justifying particular shares is *needs* rather than *contributions*. But whichever criterion one uses, the recognized social and legal legitimacy of a claim could be both a *determinant* of bargaining power and an outcome of bargaining power. Perhaps both these factors may be taken as complementary to one another towards establishing the legitimacy of a claim.

Although Sen appears to emphasize only other people's valuation of women's contribution, Agarwal extends the analysis to include a woman's own valuation of her contribution which would also be relevant. She arrives at the conclusion that it is not so much that women need to realize that they *deserve* better, but that they need to believe they *can* get a better deal, and to know how that would be possible. In other words, in explaining intra-household gender inequalities and gender gaps in measures of well-being, Agarwal places 'much less emphasis than Sen on women's perceptions of their self-interest and much more on the external constraints on their acting on those interests. Or, what may be needed is less a sharpening of women's sense of self-interest than an improvement in their ability to pursue that interest, including by strengthening their bargaining power' (Agarwal, 1994, 57). Part of this would come from improving their fall-back position, and a part from strengthening the legitimacy of their claims as perceived by others.[16]

The Household

The 'household' as a concept has significance for attempts to broaden law's consideration of rural women's claim to land ownership. In addition to anthropological perspectives of the family, feminist and economic perspectives have broadened

---

collusive solution, if different, would be more favourable to that person' (Sen, 1987, 25).

16 For a critical appraisal of this debate and its implications for gender and agency, see Kandiyoti (1998).

the scope of analyses to include the household (Agarwal, 2003). The 'family' as a structure has been studied and detailed in different aspects by anthropologists, who have questioned the concept of the 'household' as the conflation of units of residence, reproduction and production into a single unified entity. Kabeer argues that the concept of the 'household' is nevertheless relevant to analyses of distribution and allocation. She argues that

> the empirical significance of household relationships in the daily management of resource entitlements, and as a routine context of people's lives suggests that it has a certain factity despite its shifting guises (Kabeer, 1995, 114).

Legal analysis needs to incorporate analysis of women as peasants, within households. Whereas, the law, through the HSA, conceptualizes them as Hindu women within the family, this section addresses the concept of the 'household' as significant within economic analyses to extend our analysis of law.

Within the bargaining approach, the household is conceptualized as a complex matrix of relationships in which there is ongoing negotiation, subject to the social identities based on age, gender, relationship of the members. The nature of the interaction between members is characterized by both co-operation and conflict, and the members co-operate in so far as co-operative arrangements makes each better off than non co-operation. Many different co-operative outcomes are possible in relation to who does what, who gets what and how each member fares. The outcome to emerge depends on the relative bargaining power of each member, particularly defined by the strength of the person's fall-back position, and the degree to which her claim is seen as socially legitimate. The fall back position is determined by the range of outside options which would affect the member's well being if co-operation ceased (Folbre, 1986; Sen, 1987; Agarwal, 1994).

The household has emerged from changed analysis within the economic models of sharing and altruism, represented by a unity of interests, towards a recognition of the plural, conflicting interests within it, where decisions are the result of contestation and co-operation (Hart, 1995; Kabeer, 1995).[17] At the same time, analyses within feminist theory have increasingly located the family/household as the site of the women's oppression (Harris, 1981; Whitehead, 1981; Hartmann, 1987). Moore (1991) argues

> households are important in feminist analyses because they organise a large part of women's domestic/reproductive labour. As a result, both the composition and the organisation of households have a direct impact on women's lives, and on their ability to gain access to resources, to labour and to income (Moore, 1991, 55).

This combined perspective focuses on the family/household as the locus of competing interests, rights, obligations and resources, where the household members are often involved in bargaining and negotiation. The outcome of such negotiation therefore,

---

17 See Kabeer, 1995, for a clear, non-technical elaboration of the developments within and competing conceptualisations of the household within economics.

has been recognized to be determined not simply by economic factors such as access to resources, but by power and ideology (Hart, 1993; Kabeer, 1995; Moore, 1995). Socially and historically specific views about the rights, responsibilities and the need of particular individuals determine the outcome of the bargaining.

The problem of precisely how the bargaining power in the household may be significantly affected by questions of power and ideology is posed by Moore (1994). Given that the household is a permeable rather than a bounded unit, and that the workings of the household have something to do with the social, political and economic processes outside them, she argues that it is possible to comprehend the workings of the household or the links which bind them to larger scale institutions and processes only by taking into account the relations of production (Moore, 1995). She argues that the household is engaged in reciprocal relationships with the larger scale economic, political and social processes and institutions which produce social identities. In so far as social reproduction may be understood as the production and reproduction of social identities (Moore, 1995), the household may be seen as crucial to social reproduction.

The household is distinctive in that it is the site for the production of people and therefore the society, but also for the production of certain sorts of persons with specific social identities, particular rights and needs The specificity of rights and the needs of certain people is determined by various cultural and contextual evaluations, and has an impact upon the intra-household allocation of resources. Bargaining within the household, between men and women, is often about political definition of terms and interpretation of normative practices and understandings (Agarwal, 1994; Kabeer, 1995; Moore, 1995). Issues such as:

> residence rights and inheritance laws are relevant to household analysis in that they not only describe sets of social and economic relations, but also encode ideas about gender ideologies, and about the different nature, tastes and roles of the woman and man in the society. Gender ideologies are not just ideas, cultural belief and notions that are somehow related to the economic and political processes, they are constitutive of them. Hence gender ideologies and other forms of differences such as race and class, which draw on the social identities are crucial to understanding social reproduction, both at the level of the household and at the level of the state (Moore, 1995, 92).

An analysis of the gender and the household dynamics brings into issue how the household is characterized, whether as an undifferentiated unit or as an arena of both conflict and co-operation. Within the bargaining model of intra-household relations individuals are characterized by their own preferences, rather than aggregated as within the unitary conceptualization. Therefore, household behaviour should be understood explicitly as a collective process involving more than one decision unit (Hart, 1995; Kabeer, 1995).

Since assumptions regarding the household can impinge critically on policy decisions regarding whom resources and programmes are directed toward (Ginwala et al., 1990), there is a recognized need to take into account the intra-household allocation of resources (Tinker, 1991; Agarwal, 1994; Kabeer, 1995). For example, policy makers in India have (implicitly or explicitly), assumed a unitary household model and have tended to direct resources principally at male household heads, trusting that resources will be shared equitably within the household; but empirical evidence shows considerable intra-household inequities (Dyson and Moore, 1983; Agarwal, 1992; Agarwal, 1994; Kabeer, 1995; Panda, 1997; Dreze and Sen, 1999).

However, Hart points out that rather than simply shifting the focus from the household to the individuals within, there is a need to focus on *relationships* within and between households, and on the way these relationships are defined in terms of gender,

> Taking account of gender is not simply a matter of adding women, or discrimination, but an account of how multiple understandings of "male" and "female" are socially constructed and embodied in everyday practices both within and beyond the household (Hart, 1995, 40).

Gender in this sense is crucial to understanding not only *what* are the culturally variable rules governing access to and control over resources and labour, but also *how* definitions of rules, rights and obligations are reinforced, renegotiated and openly challenged (Whitehead, 1981). A key insight of this gendered politicized understanding of the household is that policies not only affect different members differently, but also may provoke renegotiations of gendered relations within and beyond the household.

Application of the Bargaining Approach

Adopting elements of the bargaining approach brought out both by Sen and Agarwal, it becomes possible to explore the gender-biased outcome in relation to access to land. The perceived interests of women, characterized in terms of maximizing 'family welfare' for their own well-being are sought to be explained in terms of the existing gender ideology that in fact excludes conceptions of their individual welfare, distinct from the family. This exclusion is derived from the ideology explicit in Hindu cultural and traditional values.

The family as a social unit is the site where these values and principles are lived out and become operationalized, as well as the site for their reproduction. Thus, Hindu understandings of the position of a woman – including her position as a daughter (not being a part of her natal family, but only her husband's family upon marriage), the status accorded to her, based upon performance of her duties and obligations as a wife, the loss of identity and entity as a widow, and the constant dependence characterized throughout her life course – form the basis upon which perceptions of the women of their own well-being are founded.

The role of legal provisions in maintaining and reinforcing these perceptions is brought out by reference to the principles of Hindu law relating to family and women's property. On the other hand, the law does not take any cognisance of, or respond to, the material reality of women's role in agriculture. Further, analysis of the material context of peasant women in small farming households requires a consideration of their role and contribution within the economic production process of which they are a part. The nature of and the size of the holding, in addition to the subsistence nature of the production, leads to the fact that a significant part of the women's role is within their own homes and the family land. This locates my analysis within the family/household.

Posing the persistent undervaluation and estimation of women's role and contribution in agriculture, in official spheres and studies, as the direct reflection of the same undervaluation within the wider society, I explore the second aspect of perceived contribution: the perception of women themselves within agriculture. In this, I draw out the links between gender ideology and the material context of Hindu peasant women to expose the difference in perceptions of others' and their own perceptions. I evaluate the effect of these factors upon negotiating access to land by analysing the effect of gender ideology, in combination with others' perceptions of women's lower contribution, to deny the legitimacy of women's access to land.

Notions embodied in cultural practices, which define what is permissible, in what contexts, within which spaces, and using what modes of conduct, are crucial to women's ability to self-manage land. They also have a significant impact upon the visibility and recognition that may be given to women's actual roles and contributions within agriculture. For example, the principle of female seclusion is rationalized in terms of family and personal honour, female chastity, modesty, and the need to control female sexuality, among others. Further, a woman's character and chastity may be associated with compliance to norms of seclusion, so that women who observe the norms are assumed to be chaste and good and those who transgress them to be of questionable moral character.

The strength of operative gender ideology to perpetuate women's exclusion from land brings out the limitation of conceptualizing women's access to land as the result of the factors operating within the bargaining approach. The overriding effect of notions of legitimacy determined by gender ideology is brought out by the perceptions of women when they say:

> Equal inheritance by brothers and sisters ... would only have one result. Brothers and sisters would quarrel. Brothers would want to obtain their sisters' shares and sisters might feel they were not adequately reimbursed. The close protective relationship of brother and sister would be in jeopardy (Agarwal, 1994, 265).

Again, laws providing for equal shares in family land were viewed as:

> a deliberate and sinister attempt to destroy the family and morality ... this equality must have the inevitable consequences of increasing divorce, desertion, adultery, destroying the love between husband and wife, depriving the children of the certainty of a normal home life, setting brother against brother, son against father, and man against man; that it would in a word, atomise society by gnawing at the foundations of the social bonds (Agarwal, 1994, 271).

Perceptions and understandings such as these are causally linked to the decreased significance of women's own perceptions of contributions in relation to increasing the legitimacy of their claims, as the basis of such a claim would militate against the ideological constructs. Thus, women's own perceptions of a higher contribution may not affect the outcome primarily because of the operation of gender ideology that is constituted upon, and constitutive of, women's exclusion from land. Notions of a greater legitimacy of desert and therefore to greater access, are in fact subject to, and limited by, the exclusion of access to land from its operation. What we have therefore, may very well be a circular argument.

This is a reflection of the issue brought out by Agarwal as she explores the effect of gender differentials in bargaining power, not only in outcomes but also *what is bargained about*. Not all issues may be accepted as legitimate ones for contestation. At any given time, for any society, some decisions would fall in the realm of:

> ... that which is accepted and a self-evident part of the social order, which goes without saying and *is not open to questioning or contestation* – the undiscussed, unnamed, admitted without argument or scrutiny (Agarwal, 1994, 58) (emphasis added).

What constitutes 'tradition' may itself be subject to challenge and change (Risseeuw, 1991) and such change would come about 'when the dominated have the material and symbolic means of rejecting the definition of the real that is imposed on them, or within the bargaining framework, when the dominated have a stronger bargaining position' (Agarwal, 1994, 59). Agarwal posits that the strength of a person's bargaining power therefore (1) is defined not only by material circumstances but also by symbolic meanings; and (2) not only affects the outcomes of bargaining over those issues/items which are admitted into the realm of contestation, but also what issues/items are so admitted. The premise is that the greater a person's ability to physically survive outside the family, the greater would be the bargaining power within the family. Inequalities based upon gender or age among family members in respect of these factors would place some members in a weaker bargaining position relative to others.

However, in my own view the strength of the approach lies in its *explanatory* potential, if not its *emancipatory* potential. It provides a framework that is grounded in culturally constituted identities, generating the means to evaluate the actual interactions between people in a relational context. It provides for a framework grounded in the interaction and operation of action within a structure, allowing us to analyse the precise ways in which each may impact the other by taking into account the individual's internalized conception of 'self-interest' as well as the externally validated notions of 'contribution' and 'desert' in order to establish legitimacy of a claim. Further, one cannot disregard its emancipatory potential in the light of the fact that the perceptions of women's contributions have not been positively enhanced, as yet, either in popular or policy terms. In this context, one may hypothesize that the approach presents a comprehensive mode for bringing issues of women's ownership of land within the realm of what may be contested.

Conclusion

In analysing the factors that affect Hindu women's ability to own land within small peasant households, it is necessary to evaluate the legal framework within which such access is framed. An understanding of the ideological background of law as it constructs 'Hindu' law and the HSA within religious discourse enables us to understand the construction of 'Hindu' women and their right to ownership through succession within this. The historical processes which structured colonial debates around 'modernity' and 'tradition' in turn reinforce the operation of religion, particularly upon the lives of women. Whereas the liberal principles of the legal and constitutional framework enable formal guarantees of equality, they also operate to exclude actual inequalities from the realm of the law. This is the result of the public/private distinction implicit within liberalism, analogous to the division maintained between family/work. This serves on the one hand, to reinforce the operation of religious ideology in women's lives, within the 'private', and to exclude from the purview of law the work that peasant women are engaged in, within the 'family'.

Thoughts developed on legal pluralism enable us to broaden the scope of law's scope and domain, allowing for the evaluation of the impact of religious norms upon women's lives, as well as the expansion of legal analysis within the household and the workplace. The breadth afforded by legal pluralism to take account of the totality of structures and processes, informed by a variety of norms, is strengthened by the arguments to contextualize law and take account of women's lives as they are actually lived.

The context of law must take account of the material aspects of women's lives in addition to the ideological, where analyses of gender and property have shown the two to be inextricably intertwined. The bargaining approach provides a framework for embarking upon an analysis which incorporates both aspects. It provides us with a framework that enables us to take account of the norms and processes that affect women's access to resources. In addition, it allows for the analysis of the interaction between the ideological and material conditions that impact upon such access.

Thus, whereas the issue of Hindu women's right to property has been framed by law in exclusively ideological terms, the bargaining approach enables us to expand the framework of law by allowing the incorporation of the material aspects of women's lives within the analysis. This allows for a more complete evaluation of the factors that affect women's ability to access property, and therefore to evolve an understanding of law which has a broader frame of vision.

Chapter 3

The Development of Females' Proprietary Rights in Hindu Law

Introduction

Hindu Law,[1] of which the law of succession forms a part, includes other areas of family life such as marriage, adoption, maintenance and guardianship. It is the personal law of Hindus as understood formerly under colonial rule, continuing to the present day. As such, it is the combination of principles of the *Shastras* as applied and administered by the colonial courts, the central and state statutes of both pre and post-independence India, and judicial decisions.

In order to evaluate the extent to which the law provides a framework for negotiating independent ownership of land for women, this chapter will discuss the legal provisions relating to the position of women, situated within the religious context. The development of codified Hindu law has been towards the incorporation of a new principle, to legitimate women's independent ownership of land. The inclusion of females' successory rights to parental property under the Hindu Succession Act (1956), introduces a principle that is a significant departure from what has traditionally been practised and upheld. At the same time, important aspects relating to these successory rights remain unchanged by the Act. Thus, it contravenes existing norms, understandings and attitudes by introducing a fundamental change and simultaneously retains other significant aspects in relation to females' rights. In doing so, it sets up a self-contradictory position, affected as it were by fundamentally opposite forces, ultimately raising issues regarding the ultimate effectiveness of the changes themselves.

Tracing briefly the statutory development of the right first, to a Hindu widow to hold a limited estate and subsequently its conversion to an absolute estate, and the inclusion of the daughter and mother as equal heirs with the sons and the widow of a Hindu male, this chapter will outline the relevant provisions and the changes sought to be effected. Included in this section will also be the provisions within the HSA which limit the rights of women. This section will also bring out the effect of the statutory developments of the Hindu law, arguing that these act as piecemeal changes, affecting only specific subject areas, and leaving a whole body of uncodified Hindu law untouched, which continue to operate along with statutory provisions.

---

1   While the focus of this chapter is on succession; for the broader subject of Hindu law within which it falls, see Derrett (1968, 1970); Kane (1968); Sen (1984); Mulla (1990); for compilation and commentary of general principles and law.

A brief history of the development of 'Hindu law' and the central role of religion has resulted in the institution of religious norms as binding law within the contemporary legal system. To the extent that enacted laws establish the legitimacy and operation of religious norms, there arises a tension when alien principles are brought within the frame of existing religious/legal norms. Law operates to perpetuate and actively sanction the practice of religious norms and values affecting the individual directly, and social institutions like the family, indirectly.

The Statutory Development of Hindu Women's Right to Property

Historical Background: Mitakshara and Dayabhaga Schools

The personal law governing Hindus in India today is 'Hindu Law', consisting of both traditional Hindu law and statutory law. It includes pre and post-independence statutes and judicial decisions as administered by courts both under British rule as well as independent India.[2] The traditional Hindu laws have been declared and interpreted through commentaries. These commentaries, have in course of time appear to have acted with ever increasing force of law. The commentators, through their opinions and conclusions, amplified narrow provisions of the law and added a mass of relevant matter that came to be understood as the law (Mulla, 1991).

The Hindu law of Succession in its traditional form remained in application throughout the country until the middle of the nineteenth century. There are two principal schools of Hindu law, the *Mitakshara* and *Dayabhaga*.[3] The *Mitakshara* law as well as the *Dayabhaga* rules were in force in various parts of the country, with the courts applying and interpreting the principles contained therein in the process outlined earlier. While the *Dayabhaga* school operated mainly in Bengal and Assam, the *Mitakshara* school was in force in the rest of the country. Both these systems of law were derived from *Shastras* and based upon digests or commentaries by sages (*Smritis*). The *Mitakshara* was based upon the commentaries of Vijnaneshwara on the *Yagnavalkya Smriti*, and the *Dayabhaga* was founded upon the text by Jimutvahana.[4]

---

2   The adoption of the Indian Constitution did not pose a break from colonial laws or judicial and administrative framework, but allowed for the continuance of these, with some exceptions: Art. 13 Constitution of India 1950.

3   Apart from the two principal schools mentioned above, reference must be made to certain systems prevailing among considerable section of people inhabiting the west coast of south India. These schools called the Marumakkattayam, Aliyasantana and Nambudri embodied a system of regulations which have received judicial recognition. These schools have largely similar principles though they do differ in certain aspects. The fundamental difference between the Marumkkattaym and the other schools of Hindu law is that it is founded on the matriarchal family and descent is from a common ancestress, whereas in the other schools descent is from a common patriarch.

4   See further Mulla and Kane for details on the two schools of Hindu law.

As explained by the Judicial Committee of the Privy Council in *Collector of Madura v Moottoo Ramalinga*:

> The remoter sources of Hindu law are common to all the different schools. The process by which those schools have developed seems to have been of this kind. Works universally or very generally received became the subject of subsequent commentaries. The commentator put his own gloss on the ancient text, and his authority having been received in one and rejected in another part of India, schools with conflicting doctrines arose. Thus the *Mitakshara* which is universally accepted by all schools except that of Bengal as of the highest authority, and which in Bengal is received also as of highest authority, yielding only to the *Dayabhaga* in those points where they differ, was a commentary on institutions of Yajnavalkya; and the *Dayabhaga*, which wherever it differs from the *Mitakshara*, prevails in Bengal, and is the foundation of the principal divergence between that and the other schools, equally admits and relies on the authority of the Yajnavalkya. In like manner there are glosses and commentaries upon the *Mitakshara*, which are received by some of the schools that acknowledge the supreme authority of that treatise, but are not received by all (Mulla, 1990, 42; italics added).

As regards property and inheritance the two schools had significant differences. The Mitakshara was based upon the coparcenary consisting of males of up to four generations, in the undivided property of which every male (coparcener) acquired an absolute interest by birth. The amount of this individual interest fluctuated with births and deaths of coparceners, and could be determined at any time only by partition from the coparcenary, to become his separate property. However, until such partition, the property was held jointly as joint family property and included property inherited from male ancestors as well as any separate property that was pooled by an individual coparcener into the joint family property. Devolution of property was thus by survivorship and there were many restrictions on the powers of alienation of joint family property. Rights of disposal over separate property were, however, absolute. The separate property included self-acquired property, as well as property inherited from persons other than direct male ancestors. In the presence of male descendants extending to four generations, property inherited from direct male ancestors as well as the person's own share in the joint family upon partition became joint family property and subject to the same restrictions regarding alienation.

Under the *Dayabhaga* system, males did not acquire a right by birth and division of shares could take place only upon the death of the owner. The owner had absolute rights over all his property and was able to dispose of it as he wished. Devolution was not by survivorship and each heir took a definite share.

Under the Mitakshara, women could not become coparceners, hence they did not have a right in the joint family property by birth. However, they were entitled to be maintained by their male relatives as wives, widows or unmarried daughters, the last being entitled to marriage expenses and associated gifts. A widow could inherit a limited estate of her husband's separate property in some circumstances (the absence of any of the following: sons, agnatic grandsons and agnatic great-grandsons), and on condition of chastity. A daughter's claim, again to a limited estate, came after the widow's, and an unmarried daughter was preferred to a married one. Thus, a daughter could claim a share in her father's property only in the absence of both a mother and the listed male heirs.

Under the *Dayabhaga*, property of a male was to go in the first instance equally to his sons, or, the share of one predeceased to devolve upon his male lineal descendants. On the absence of these males alone could a chaste widow inherit a limited estate. The daughters came after the widow, again unmarried ones receiving preference over married ones. However, women under the Dayabhaga inherited an interest in all property, separate and joint family.

Statutory Changes Leading to The Hindu Succession Act, 1956

From the above, it is clear that under customary Hindu Law women did not have any substantial claim in the inheritance of property, and even in the remote occasions where they could inherit, it was only a limited estate. The first statutory enactment to directly impact upon this position of women in the matter of inheritance was the Hindu Women's Right to Property Act of 1937. The effect of the Act was to include the widow, predeceased son's widow and widow of predeceased son of a predeceased son as entitled to a share in the property of the male they survived. However, this share was only a limited estate. The next major change regarding the proprietary interest of Hindu females was through the provisions of the Hindu Succession Act, 1956. The Act has overriding application in respect of any of the matters dealt with in the Act and repeals all existing laws inconsistent with it.[5] However, it does not touch or affect the law relating to joint family and partition and the previous law continues to operate in such matters.[6]

The law of inheritance by which Hindus are governed today is the HSA. It was enacted in order to codify and amend the law in relation to intestate succession among Hindus and to give effect to equal rights to both female and male heirs. It sought to improve upon the position created by the Hindu Women's Right to Property Act (1937), under which widows for the first time became entitled to an estate.[7] This estate was only a limited one, however, and the widow could not dispose of it according to her will. The Act of 1956 provides for the property of a female to be her absolute property.[8]

A brief outline of the specific changes brought about by the HSA is provided below. For purposes of clarity, it should be borne in mind that among the two main schools of Hindu law discussed earlier the Mitakshara is most widely prevalent.

---

5   Section 4, HSA.

6   Thus, for instance the right of the mother or widow to a share on partition between the father and sons in a Mitakshara family or between the sons after the death of the father is not affected or abrogated by this Act. *Gopal Narain v D.P. Goenka (71) A. Delhi 61.*

7   Section 3, Hindu Women's Right to Property Act (1937).

8   Section 14, HSA

Successory Rights of Females in Mitakshara Coparcenary Property

The HSA provides for succession of property by the female or a male heir, claiming through such a female, although its provisions are not applicable to succession of Mitakshara coparcenary property. Under Section 6 the law is stated as follows:

> when a male Hindu dies after the commencement of this Act, having at the time of his death an interest in a Mitakshara coparcenary property, his interest shall devolve by survivorship upon the surviving members of the coparcenery and not in accordance with this Act:

> provided that, if the deceased has left him a surviving a female relative specified in Class I of the Schedule or a male relative, specified in that class who claims, through such female relative, the interest of the deceased in the Mitakshara coparcenery property shall devolve by testamentary or intestate succession, as the case may be, under this Act and not by survivorship.

Although this section deals with succession, it has bearing on other branches of Hindu law such as joint family, adoption and maintenance and lays downs rules of far reaching consequences. It prescribes that where a coparcener dies, the Mitakshara coparcenary will not become disrupted but the surviving coparceners may continue to remain members of the joint family without arriving at any partition and subject to the important proviso engrafted on the rule, the undivided interest of any coparcener in any coparcenary property will upon his death devolve by survivorship upon the surviving coparceners.

The order of devolution of property of a male Hindu dying intestate includes the daughter, widow, mother, daughter of a predeceased son, widow of a predeceased son, daughter of a predeceased daughter, daughter of a predeceased son of a predeceased son and widow of a predeceased son of a predeceased son.[9]

Absolute Ownership

Under the Hindu law in operation before the coming into force of the HSA a woman's ownership of property was limited with regard to her rights of disposal by acts inter vivos and also her testamentary power in respect of that property. Absolute power of alienation was held only in property obtained from certain sources. Her rights over property were understood depending upon her status as a maiden, married woman or widow.

Section 14 of the HSA overrides the old law in respect of all property possessed by the woman and declares that all such property shall be held by her as a full owner. The Act confers a full heritable capacity on the female heir and this section dispenses with the traditional limitations on the powers of a female Hindu to hold and Transmit property. Under this section, limited ownership where it existed is converted into absolute ownership. The consequence of the altered law is to affect the incidents of

---

9   Section 8, HSA.

women's property, not only in respect of property that might be acquired and held by her after the coming into force of the Act but also in respect of property that might be acquired by her in the past and possessed by her.

For example, the undivided interest of the husband in the joint family property devolved upon the widow immediately on the death of the husband, and she would be in possession of the property. The effect of the Section 14 is to transform that statutory interest of the widow of which she was a limited owner into that of a full owner. That fact she had not sought partition before the present Act came into force in 1956 made no difference. Similarly where at the time of her death the widow was in possession of her share of property to which she was entitled under the Hindu Women's Right to Property Act, 1937, that share or that property would devolve upon her heirs and the latter would be entitled to prosecute a suit for partition filed by the woman (Mulla, 1990).

Position of Widow, Daughter and Mother

The widow of a male Hindu inherits simultaneously with a son, daughter and the other heirs specified above.[10] The share of the property taken by her under the Act is absolute and not as a widow's estate, by the application and operation of Section 14 of the Act. If there are more widows than one then all the widows together, take one share. The old law has also been changed, in so far as unchastity of a widow is, under the Act, no longer a ground for disqualifying her from succeeding to the estate of her husband. Further, under the provisions of this Act, remarriage of the widow is not a ground for divesting the estate inherited by her from her husband. The Hindu Widow Remarriage Act, 1856, though it legalized the remarriage of widows, had the effect of divesting the estate inherited by her as a widow. By her second marriage she forfeited her interest taken by her in her first husband's estate, and it passed to the next heirs of her husband as if she was dead. The rule laid down in that enactment is not applicable to a case governed by the HSA and the widow becomes the full owner of the share of interest in her husband's property that may devolve on her under the provisions of this Act. Her remarriage, which would evidently be after the vesting in her of her share of interest on the death of the husband, would not operate to divest such share or interest. The widow of a predeceased son inherits simultaneously with a son, widow and other heirs specified in Class I of the Schedule. She is, however, not entitled to succeed if, on the date of the succession, she has remarried.

The daughter, whether married or unmarried, inherits simultaneously with a son, widow and the other heirs specified in Class I of the Schedule. Each daughter takes one share which is equal to that of a son. She takes her share as an absolute share and not as woman's estate. Further, there is no priority between married and unmarried daughters, signalling another major change from the customary law where unmarried daughters were given preference over married ones.

The mother inherits along with the son, widow, daughter and other heirs specified in Class I of the Schedule. She also takes her share absolutely. Unchastity of the mother is no bar to her succeeding as heir to her son; nor does divorce or remarriage

---

10 Section 9, op. cit.

constitute any such bar. Sections 4 and 14 of the HSA clearly establish that the remarriage of the mother is no bar to the mother inheriting as an heir of the son and there can be no divesting of the interest that she acquires in his property by reason of remarriage. This includes adoptive mothers because under the old Hindu law and now under the Hindu Adoption and Maintenance Act, 1956, an adopted son is deemed to be the child of the adoptive parent or parents for all purposes with effect from the date of adoption.

Retention of Mitakshara Coparcenary

The Hindu law of inheritance evolved subsequent to the joint family system, and applied to property held in absolute severalty as distinguished from property held by the joint family. A Hindu joint family is comprised of all persons lineally descended through males from a common ancestor, and includes their wives and unmarried daughters. A daughter ceases to be a member of her father's family on marriage and becomes a member of her husband's family. A joint or undivided Hindu family may, for example, consist of a single male member and widows of deceased male members, or a male Hindu, his wife and unmarried daughter, or a male Hindu and his wife, or even two female members. Within this operated, in the Mitakshara, the coparcenary consisting of males of up to four generations, in the undivided property of which every male (coparcener) acquired an absolute interest by birth.

Before the enactment of the HSA and during the debates around the Hindu Code Bill, it was felt by certain sections that radical reforms was required in the Mitakshara law of coparcenary. In particular, it was felt that where one of the coparceners died it was necessary that not only in case of his separate property but also in respect of his undivided interest in the coparcenary property there should be an equal distribution of that share between the male and female heirs and particularly between the daughters and the sons.[11]

The HSA prescribes that where a coparcener dies intestate the Mitakshara coparcenary does not necessarily become disrupted. According to the notion of the undivided family governed by the Mitakshara law, no individual member of the coparcenary, whilst the family remains joint and undivided, can predicate, of the joint family property, that he has a definite share in the same. His interest is a fluctuating interest, capable of being enlarged by deaths in the family and liable to be diminished by births in the family. It is only on partition that he becomes entitled to a definite share.

The HSA does not interfere with the rights of the members of a Mitakshara coparcenary. Nevertheless, without abolishing joint family property, it recognizes, upon the death of a coparcener, the right of certain preferential heirs to claim an interest in the property that would have allotted to such coparcener if a partition of the joint family property had in fact taken place immediately before his death. Such preferential heirs, to mention some, are the daughter, the predeceased daughters son and the predeceased sons daughter.

---

11 Section 10, op. cit.

The section proceeds first by making provision for the retention of the right by survivorship and then engrafting on this rule the qualification noted above. The initial part of the section ('... shall devolve by survivorship') stresses that the HSA does not interfere with the special rights of those who are members of Mitakshara coparcenary except where the deceased has left him surviving a daughter's son or any female heir specified in Class I of the schedule.[12] Thus, intended to be remedial and beneficial, the proviso to the section confers new rights upon the specified female heirs only by superimposing upon the integrated structure of the law relating to the Mitakshara coparcenary.

Probably, the best solution would have been to abolish the ancient legal formulae of acquisition by right of birth and devolution by survivorship under Mitakshara law and adopt the Dayabhaga system of the joint family. As noted earlier, the difference between these systems in respect of ownership and succession to property is significant. The Mitakshara recognizes two modes of devolution of property, namely, survivorship and succession. While the rule of survivorship applies to joint family coparcenary property (not subject to the rules under this Act), the rules of succession apply only to property held in absolute severalty, or separate property. Most significantly, whereas the ownership of the coparcenary property is in the whole body of coparceners and the essence of a coparcenary under the Mitakshara law is the unity of ownership, females are completely excluded from this. No female can be a coparcener under the Mitakshara law; a wife is not her husband's coparcener, nor is a mother a coparcener with the sons.

On the other hand, the Dayabhaga recognizes only one mode of devolution, namely succession and does not recognize the rule of survivorship even in case of joint family property. The reason is that no member of the family has a right by birth and every member of a Dayabhaga family holds his share in *quasi*-severalty. This passes on at his death to his heirs as if he was absolutely seized thereof, and not to the surviving coparceners as under the Mitakshara law.

This would have also achieved the desired goal of bringing about uniformity in the diverse principles of Hindu law operative throughout the country by assimilating the Mitakshara to the Dayabhaga in this respect. It would also have the merit of equable treatment of the nearest female heirs of a coparcener. When moving the Hindu Succession Bill, referring to the Rau Committee's recommendations, Pataskar, Minister for Law, observed[13]:

> ... To retain the Mitakshara joint family and at the same time to put the daughter on the same footing as a son with respect to the right by birth, right of survivorship and to claim partition at any time, will be to provide for a joint family unknown to the law and unworkable in practise .... In the circumstances ... the Rau Committee came to the only possible conclusion that hereafter ... the law need recognise only one form of joint family, namely, the joint family, known as the Dayabhaga system of law. In this matter, I would be willing to be guided by the wishes of the house ... (4 Lok Sabha Debates, 1955: Col. 8014).

---

12 This is done by introducing the concept of a notional partition immediately before his death and the carving out of his share in the coparcenary property as of that date.

13 4 Lok Sabha Debates, col. 8014 (1955).

The Rau Committee considered the retention of the Mitakshara coparcenary and suggested conversion of the Mitakshara and Dayabhaga coparcenary. The decision of the house was to retain the Mitakshara coparcenary and to confer on the daughters and the other female members, mentioned in class I of the schedule, the right to share the undivided interest of the deceased coparcener. It appears that the main consideration that prompted the committee at arriving at its decision is the uniformity in the Hindu law that would be achieved by the measure rather than promotion of equality of sexes.[14]

The HSA has been amended by legislation in various states to provide for women to become a coparceners in a Mitakshara coparcenary. For example, the Hindu Succession (Andhra Pradesh Amendment) Act 1986 confers on daughters the rights in coparcenary properties and is an important statute in the post-Independence legislations affecting the joint Hindu family. It incorporates views which were discarded as 'unknown to the law and unworkable in practise' three decades earlier. The principle on which the Andhra Pradesh amendment relies is that of equality as enshrined in the Indian Constitution. It is intended the amendment will better the condition of the women in the Hindu society (Sivaramayya, 1988). Similar amendments to the HSA have been made in Karnataka[15] and Tamil Nadu.[16] Kerala, on the other hand, has abolished the joint family itself through the Kerala Joint Hindu Family (Abolition) Act 1975. Most recently, the Hindu Succession (Amendment) Act 2005 extended this change to include daughters as coparceners to the whole country. The Act came into effect on September 9 2005 and although promulgated with the expressed aim of removing inequalities within the 1956 Act, raises further questions on the rights of Hindu women as will be discussed in the following sections.

Females' Property and Succession Thereto

Section 15 presents a scheme of succession to the property of a female Hindu who dies intestate after the commencement of the Act. The section groups heirs of a female intestate into five categories. Sons, daughters, children of any predeceased son or daughter and her husband are the heirs specified under the first entry taking simultaneously and to the exclusion of those specified under the subsequent entries. Failing all heirs of the intestate female specified in the above, her property devolves upon the heirs of her husband. These are preferred to those in the next category, namely the mother and father of the intestate. On failure of the mother or father the property devolves upon the heirs of the father and in case of failure of all the previously listed heirs, upon the heirs of the mother.

---

14 Report of the Hindu Law Committee 57 (1947). Clause 7, rule 4 says: 'Each surviving daughter of an intestate shall take half a share whether she is unmarried, married or a widow.'

15 The Hindu Succession Act, Karnataka (Amendment) Act 1994, which came into force on 30 July 1994.

16 The Hindu Succession (Tamil Nadu) Amendment Act 1990.

However, there are two important exceptions to the general order of succession enacted in the five entries. The exception relates to the property inherited by the female from her father or mother and property inherited by her from her husband or father-in-law. In case of a female intestate dying without issue property inherited by her from the father or mother will revert to the heirs of the father in existence at the time of her death and not upon the husband or the heirs of the husband in accordance with the general order of succession laid down in the entries. Similarly in case of a female intestate dying without issue, property inherited by her from her husband or father-in-law (as widow of a predeceased son) will revert to the heirs of the husband in existence at the time of her death and not upon the heirs of the father or mother in accordance with the general order of succession laid down in the entries.

Testamentary Succession

A coparcener under the Mitakshara law has no power to dispose of his coparcenary interest by gift. However, the extension of this principle, which disentitled a coparcener to make a bequest of his interest in the coparcenary property so as to defeat the rights of the other members to take by survivorship, is now abolished.[17] Thus, any Hindu male or female may now dispose of by will or other testamentary disposition in accordance with the provisions of the Indian Succession Act, 1925, or any other law relating to such dispositions applicable to Hindus. This power of testamentary disposition is subject to the rights of maintenance of persons who are entitled to claim maintenance as dependants of the testator or testatrix.

Summary: An Overall Change in Females' Position under HSA?

The above brief outline of the relevant provisions regarding the position of females in Hindu law as changed by the Hindu Succession Act of 1956 may suffice to make some observations on the extent to which change has in fact been attempted. In considering and evaluating the present law governing intestate succession, the traditional foundation and historical operation must be kept in mind, in addition to considerations of constitutional principles of gender and social equality and progress.

As has been discussed earlier, the context within which the law operates is the joint Hindu family in which property interest passed primarily through males. This is substantiated and perpetuated through the continuation of the Mitakshara coparcenary. Therefore, although females of the description within the section initially acquired an equal share in the property of a Hindu dying intestate, and now have a share in the joint family property by birth as coparceners, this raises some issues.

This change does not apply to self-acquired property, from which a female may continue to be excluded by a valid will. Jaisingh (2005) has argued that the reforms are self-defeating to the extent that measures to increase equality cannot be simply

---

17 Section 30

grafted onto a complex body of structures and rules that make up Hindu Law. In real terms, the changes to provide a right to daughters as coparceners will have the effect of reducing the share of others, including the mother and widow, who inherit the shares of their deceased spouses. This increases the scope for greater conflict between women within a single family. In a context of growing violence against women where they are being subjected to pressure by the husband to claim her share of property, this amendment has the potential to exacerbate the dangers. As she argues,

> It is birthright in Hindu law that is the root of the problem. Birthright by definition is a conservative institution, belonging to the era of feudalism, coupled as it was with the rule of primogeniture and the inalienability of land. When property becomes disposable and self-acquired, different rules of succession have to apply. It is in the making of those rules that gender justice has to be located. What the proposed amendment does is to reinforce the birthright without working out its consequences for all women (Jaisingh, 2005).

The right of a daughter to acquire a right by birth also raises questions regarding its enforcement in the context of a society where the female was traditionally excluded almost entirely from property ownership. In such a context, a regime may popularly be perceived to be unjust where it allows a female to have a 'double benefit' to the extent that she has a right by birth as a daughter in her natal family but also acquires a right as widow in her marital family. To the extent that it may be perceived by society as unjust, its legitimacy will be eroded and efficacy reduced.

The power to dispose of property through testamentary succession in effect provides for a means to deviate from the principle of enabling females to share equally in succession to the property. This has in fact, led to what is now acknowledged to be a common means of ensuring that property does not in fact pass to females.

The Central Role of Religion in the Development of Hindu Law

Although the dual basis of Hindu law is envisaged as complementary and not contradictory and the traditional Hindu law may be modified or abrogated by statute, a hierarchy is created where statutory laws may have created new rights and obligations or altered the existing structures in certain cases. Where the society living in accordance with traditional Hindu laws and having absorbed it within their family and social structures is faced with a new statutory norm, the introduced norm may be perceived as alien.

Hindu society reflects a deep rooted adherence to values based on the precepts and fundamental principles of the religion. The conceptions and propositions contained in the various *Shastras* or *Smritis* continue to operate, be understood and propagated, even after centuries have passed. As Parasher notes, religion clearly has a positive function in Hindu society, as norms and values derived from it affect the everyday lives of Indian women in very tangible ways (Parasher, 1992).

The central role of Hindu philosophy and religion in providing a substantive and far-reaching normative framework of rights, responsibilities and obligations within Indian society is exhaustively and thoroughly brought out in the works on Menski and Derrett in particular. In his erudite and critical examination of the development and pertinent role of Hindu law in contemporary society, Menski writes:

> Indian laws in all their various manifestations are strongly rooted in Hindu concepts, just as English law is culture-specific, or French law is ideationally linked to certain foundational concepts .... Today, the concepts and rules of Hindu law are still in evidence wherever we care to look ... More or less informally, and indeed often invisibly, concepts of Hindu law continue to govern hundreds of millions of people, not only in India, but wherever Hindus, as members of the huge transnational and global Hindu diaspora, have settled (Menski, 2003, 25–26).

Derrett (1970) argues that the ideas to be found in the *Shastra* are abandoned on the surface, but the attitude of mind and conception of life are the same as those expressed in the sacred literature. This literature continues to be believed and accepted because the beliefs they express are the real attitudes, inherited leanings and group aspirations of many people; all the features of the Hindu understandings are voiced in the literature where customs, usage, ethics, philosophy, superstition, religion and fantasy combine (Derrett, 1970).

The moral and factual legitimacy of religious norms as binding is rooted in the Hindu concept of *Dharma*. The concept of Law is founded upon moral principles drawn from the *Shastras* as expositions of *Dharma* and contained a teaching of righteousness as an inherent constituent (Baxi, 1986). Although the concept of *Dharma* or righteousness is not rigid, and communities may have vastly differing customs and practices, it nevertheless pervades Hindu society. *Dharma* is also based upon *Sadacara* or 'appropriate behaviour' in the given context of any given social reality, where shared norms shape interactions of members of communities with each other and within themselves (Derrett, 1968; Menski, 2003). The textual and reflexive processes embodied in the *Shastras* and *Sadacara* respectively, together help determine the correctness of an individual's action. The binding nature and normative force of such apparently flexible concepts is nevertheless real. As Menski explains, albeit in a discussion of the sources of Hindu law:

> The important point is therefore that it is not the state which determines the rules of human co-existence in traditional Hindu law; rather, it is the social norms as crystallized in the concept of 'good behaviour' (sadacara), tested against Dharma and virtually embodying it, which provide the ultimate yardstick ... (Menski, 2003, 31).

The significance of religious precepts as they affect any satisfactory understanding of their role and impact as normative forces are described by Derrett thus:

> This attention to religious requirement is not merely as a question of mindfulness of the honours traditionally due to deceased ancestors, and to the *devas* and the other spirits benign or less benign .... It is the question of mindfulness that there are unseen forces having a constant relation to our lives. Belief in an almighty power, or "God" is an important sanction, and self-discipline, which is considered the best discipline, is all

the more effective by the operation of this superstitious or religious sanction. Thus, for example, a person will abstain from doing things that would violate the moral principles, such as stealing what could be easily stolen, because evil will befall him as *Dharma* is violated, continuing through his many rebirths (Derrett, 1968, 36).

Here religion is not taken to be the personal belief system of an individual alone, although it may be existent, but in the aspect where it is not confined to personal belief. Speaking of the Hindu religion, in particular, it is essential to note that it is a social phenomenon, irrespective of personal belief, where the character or right to perform a religious observance depends upon factual membership of a social group (Derrett, 1968; Madan, 1979). One might say that all that appears to be social is in fact religious, and all that appears to be religious is in fact social (Dumont, 1970). Further, as Srinivas writes, the practice of the Hindu religion is largely dependent for its perpetuation on such social institutions as the caste, joint family and village community and it may even be inseparable from them (Srinivas, 1967).

The development of Hindu law is reflective of a process whereby *shastric* principles embodied in the Hindu *Shastras* and religious texts became instituted as legal rules Derrett (1968); Madan (1979); Menski (2003). Under British rule, the administration of justice was based upon the scriptural texts of the Hindus and Muslims. Hindus were to be administered on issues of inheritance, marriage, caste and other religious institutions or usages according to the laws of the *Shastras*[18] (Jain, 1966). The dominance of religious sanction as the legitimizing principle for reform of Hindu law has been brought out in great depth by many writers (Mani, 1990; Oldenberg 1990; Heimsath, 1964; Nair, 1993; Chakravarty, 1998, 1990). It is now generally accepted that the reliance was in fact on the customs and traditions as practised mainly by the Brahmins, and that the process of institutionalizing Hindu law led to the official privileging the shastric texts over local custom (Derrett, 1968; Madan, 1979; Chakravarty, 1990, 1998; Nair, 2000; Menski, 2003). The supremacy of religious prescription as the basis for law remained in both its application through judicial decisions and statutory reform in the colonial period.

The post-colonial adherence to this position is reflected in the continued existence of separate personal laws of Hindus, Muslims, Christians and Parsis, notwithstanding the Constitutional declaration of secularism as one of the fundamental principles of the State in the Preamble,[19] the guarantees of equality regardless of religion,[20] among others, and the express objective of a Uniform Civil Code.[21] The case of *State of Bombay v Narasu Appa Mali*,[22] where the Supreme Court held that personal laws do not fall within the scope of 'law' within the Fundamental Rights chapter of the Constitution, makes clear that the foundational principle for these 'laws' continues to

---

18 The Plan of 1772, issued by Warren Hastings, laid down that 1. *Shastris*, or those learned in the Shastras, were to be responsible for the reporting of the law and the sentence therefrom, and 2. the *Shastris* must be consulted for the adjudication of any matter with the 'listed' subjects.

19 Preamble, *Constitution of India 1950.*

20 Article 14, op. cit.

21 Article 44, op. cit.

22 AIR 1952 Bom. 84

be religion, and not constitutional principles, even where there might be an express contravention of the latter by the former. Again, the debates in Parliament at the time of discussing the proposed Hindu Code Bill in the 1940s and 1950s reflect the sought legitimacy of law in religion.

The development of the HSA reveals that the efforts to address the particular issue of females' property rights have been bound by the tension to retain, embody and reflect the overall structure and premises of traditional Hindu law, as well as the attempt to change particular aspects within it. As Parasher notes,

> Though India has not imported foreign laws for the family and religious institutions, it is nevertheless true that the modern state legislations incorporate principles that are quite contrary to the principles in traditional jurisprudence, particularly in aspects relating to women (Parasher, 1992, 31).

Conclusion

This discussion of the contemporary law relating to succession under the Hindu Succession Act has brought out the statutory framework within which women's claim to land ownership has been addressed within Hindu law. The provisions are addressed to Hindu women, and their claim is framed as a right to succession. Such succession is to property owned by the family, with the emphasis on parental property. The provisions within this framework derive their content from religious norms, incorporated within and to some extent codified through judicial decisions. The HSA clearly reflects the religious, ideological basis upon which Hindu women's claim to land is constructed.

A narrow critique of the Act clearly shows that various provisions would be contrary in effect, where some particular provisions would limit the application of others. The Act also presents a conflict with regard to underlying principles. The retention of the Mitakshara coparcenary reiterates the fundamental division drawn within traditional Hindu law between males and females in respect of property rights. The continuance of this is antithetical to females' proprietary rights, yet this is precisely where the law attempts to locate its introduction of the same. The responses of women in the field, presented in Chapter 4, clearly reflect their lack of acceptance of females' rights to parental property within the traditional family structure. To the extent this structure corresponds to the underlying framework of the Hindu family upheld by the law, it overrides the effect of the introduced changes.

Further, by locating the changes to females' property rights within the family, the law overlooks possibilities that may be less self-conflicting. Property rights of women within their marital family are at present only available to them as widows. This represents a limitation of the right, conceived not only with respect to the husband's property alone, but coming into being only upon his death. The discussions with women in the field show that whereas they are unable to accept their rights vis-à-vis parental property, they would argue for a share in the property of their marital family that is not limited to a widow's share of her husband's property. This brings out the need for law to incorporate this and develop a regime of marital property. Indeed, the application of the HSA has been held to incorporate a Hindu widow's right to maintenance as an independent, absolute right. In the case of *V. Tulsamma v V. Sesha Reddy*[23] the court held that the pre-existing right of a Hindu widow to maintenance was transferred into independent property after the HSA came into being, with the result that this right was enforceable against the joint family property. Although this has potentially grave implications for the safety of a widow who wishes to make a claim against the joint family property, it must be seen as protecting the right to maintenance within the joint family. In this regard, it does establish a particular claim for widows within marital property.

Nevertheless, the point that remains is that this right is derived from the principles of maintenance. The basis for an independent, absolute right drawn from the right to maintenance is, although welcome, not adequate. It is inadequate to the extent that whereas every system of law, including Hindu Law, frames the right of maintenance as subject to conditions, the concept of marital joint property is the only basis for an unconditional right to property. Further, the right to maintenance is imbued with the particular role and definition of each spouse within marriage. As such, the history of maintenance rights for wives/widows has developed within the specific notions of dependence, destitution and fairness or equity. On the other hand, a regime of marital joint property needs to, and can only be created with the notion of equality between the spouses. This is what needs to be developed.

Hindu law has developed to incorporate a new value and create a new role for Hindu women as independent owners of land. Following upon a discussion of perceptions of legitimacy fundamentally shaped and constructed by religious and cultural values in the next chapter, Chapter 5 will locate the roles within the family applicable to Hindu women. Within these, the specific norms and values implicit or explicit for the fulfilment of those roles, and the extent to which the law does provide a framework for negotiating the incorporation of a new value and creation of a new role will be critically assessed.

---

23 AIR 1977 SC 1944.

Chapter 4

Conversations: What Women Think

Introduction

This chapter presents women's responses as they elaborate upon and substantiate understandings of themselves as Hindu women who have a legal right to own family land through succession. Through their own words, it highlights women's evaluations of their claim to land, their conceptualization and understandings of their role as peasants, perceptions of their work and contribution to agriculture and their perceived claim to land. It explores the understandings which women themselves have of their rights, both societal and legal. It also includes women's own assessment of their contribution to the family both through work on the land and other duties performed in the household, to determine, if any, the correlation that is made by them between work done and a claim to land ownership.

It is not in question that there has been gender progressive legislation in India.[1] But the question which remains unanswered is to what extent these have actually empowered women either through increasing actual control and ownership of property or through deepening the legitimacy and acceptability of such a claim in women's perceptions. In attempting to answer this, it becomes important to analyse women's perceptions of their location within the family and society, and their consequent relation to the wider material and ideological structures.

Within the prevalent norms of traditional Hindu society, there is an implicit, and often explicit, conjunction of women's roles and position with that of the family, caste and other social structures. The strongest expression of this may be found regarding the concept of 'honour'; the family's 'honour' resides in its female members. The interest of the family overrides the individual interest and within the family the interests of the woman are subservient to the interest of the family. One of the common factors underlying the understanding of all the women interviewed in the sample group was that, since they perceived their interest to be the interest of the family as a whole, it was beyond their comprehension as to why they should have any 'individual' self-interest. It becomes imperative, therefore, to understand women's perception of the family, parents, husband, sons and daughters.

Feminist writers and researchers have for a long time raised questions regarding the value that societies attribute to women's role and the way in which this affects their status. In the context of rural India, women's status is affected by a variety of factors, including caste, religious beliefs, social structures as well as poverty and

---

1   The range of legislations addressed to removal of gender injustice is wide. Prominent among these are those relating to dowry, dowry-deaths, inheritance and succession, rape, obscenity, sex trafficking and prostitution.

exclusion from the processes of decision making. While these factors may be seen to be operating upon women's lives to create a certain position, they may also be seen as the experiences and understandings of individual women.

Through their own expressions the following discussion presents women's understanding and experiences in relation to certain aspects of their lives, in particular, upon ownership of land by women, individual or self-interest as distinct from the family and their role in the family's survival and well being. Given that the rights within the HSA are addressed to the individual woman as the subject, there is an implicit assumption of an individual interest which the right seeks to protect. This raises the issue whether there exists an understanding, individually and collectively, of peasant women's own independent and individual self-interest.

Identity: A Question of 'Hindu', Woman and Worker?

The experience of gender as it operates to exclude women's land ownership is conceptualized around three broad issues: firstly, the meanings, boundaries and determinants of their gender identity or, what it was to them to be female; secondly, the relations between gender and land ownership if any; and third, the relation between gender identity, land ownership and work contribution, if any. The voices of women, of their perceptions of their *individual* experiences and realities provides the perspective of the contextual analysis in this book. It is a perspective that insists that the proper development of law as a means of effecting change must begin with the study of law in its social context. Women's own experiences of what constitutes their realities, therefore, provides the basis for analysing their claim to land as framed within law. This includes more specifically, a description, analysis and discussion of the ways in which the reality of women's lives informs law. In other words, law's problematic must have peoples' lived realities and experiences at its core (Maguire, 1987). Thus, the discussion of gendered access to resources as a problem for law primarily revolves around the experience of gendered exclusion. It addresses the structures and frameworks that determine or influence such exclusion, and the principles, norms or values that provide the foundational base and support for the operation of these frameworks.

This enquiry into the relationship between women's property rights and empowerment was the outcome of my own personal history and experiences.[2] As my own understanding of my experiences developed, aspects of gender as a means of establishing social relations became clearer.[3] Within the specific context

---

2   In narrating my own experiences, I acknowledge the relevance of Helen Robert's note, that '… providing the background within which a piece of research is conceived and developed … makes explicit the paradigms within which the research is set' (Roberts, 1995, 17).

3   I have always keenly felt the 'distinctiveness' of being female in my society where, more often than not, I perceived this distinctiveness to place me at a disadvantage. My earliest memories are of being quite outraged (as much as a girl of five could be!) at being told that I could not do things, like go out and play cricket with 'the boys' even though 'the boys' were my elder brother and his friends. Or, of the time when my cousin's wedding was being

of my location in a family with predominantly rural ties, also having access to good education, lower middle class but with prospects for upward mobility, gender was experienced through various practices and their implicit, but often explicitly stated, values. Practices within the family such as limited segregation, female-specific rituals and observances, as well as public experiences such as concerning personal safety, movement and even celebrations such as festivals, were underlined by specific values, ideals and roles attributed to being female.

Gender, then, is constructed through defining values and ideals in the given society, upon which roles are fostered and gender identity is developed primarily through the successful inculcation of these in the person. The experience of gender thereafter becomes inextricably linked with these values, and this is the site upon which further meanings, interactions and experiences can then be negotiated within various contexts. The family, the caste group/community, society or the state may become the site where issues such as access to education, health, personal freedom, safety, marriage and reproduction, to point out a few, are experienced specific to one's gender.

The question that arises is: what does that experience actually *mean* to those who experience it in a given context? How do any set of values that might be operative function to influence or affect what one may construe as a 'gendered' experience to make it so? Further, is there any other aspect of gender, as it was experienced, that could reverse the order? In other words, is there any potential to evolve new values, based upon gender as it is in fact experienced, which may in turn become another value in the social construction of gender? Thus, this study has been of twofold purpose for me: that of understanding the gender hierarchy in rural Indian society, and of exploring the possibilities of transforming it. Although the transformative potential of qualitative field research has been argued as desirable and even essential by some researchers, particularly feminist researchers (Mies, 1982, 1986, 1988), I am quite clear that my research was but the first, necessary step towards understanding.[4]

I begin with the understanding that women's lives in rural peasant society present the interface between their culturally constructed identities as female and as major contributors to production from land. Although one could gain documented information on the predominant role of women in agriculture, the sight of women's work in agriculture is plain to see even for the casual visitor in village India. Women are vital and productive workers in the Indian economy. However, the social construction of gender in India hinders access to resources for women, since the question of who gets what is closely linked to gender. Access is

---

discussed and the talk was about the people who were coming to 'see' her as the first step. My reaction is clear in my memory (and in my parents' it appears). I asked aloud, 'Are girls like cows in the market, that people come to "see" them?' Things only became worse after that as I grew up, as for any other girl that I knew of. The things I could not do became more in number at the same time that the things I was *supposed to do* increased too. The reason, that I was a girl, although not explicitly stated at first, was stated more and more, particularly in response to a defiant challenge.

4   See Gunsell Berik's account of her research in rural Turkey for a similar conceptualisation (Berik 1996).

related to the very meaning of male and female, and part of the culture's definition of the woman is her association with the 'inside', or the home, while men belong to the 'outside', where the livelihoods are earned and political and economic power is exercised. This social construction of gender is embedded in the interlocking religious, economic and kinship structures which define the social domain of the men and women.

On the basis of women's high level of work participation and contribution to agricultural production, a crucial question for exploration is the extent to which one facet of identity interacts with another such that both are changed by the interaction. More concretely in the context of this discussion, what is inter-relation and interaction between women's identity as agricultural labourers and producers and their culturally constructed as Hindu on the question of independent land ownership? It is clear that the primary legal instrument establishing the right to such ownership for Hindu women, the Hindu Succession Act, has been effective only to a marginal extent in increasing women's access to property. It is therefore crucially important to develop a perspective which locates the experiences and perceptions of the women to who rights within the law were addressed as central to any analysis.

Illiteracy, poverty, inaccessibility of the courts and other administrative institutions, and ignorance of the law in particular, are common exclusionary factors operative upon a majority of the people in India, particularly in rural areas. While the relevance and significance of these factors cannot be diminished, it is an additional, yet different set of factors and circumstances which interact with the above in a way to further marginalize and dispossess women. Is there a more fundamental barrier to legal effectiveness of property rights, relating to women's perception of their entitlements particularly when the resource is land? To what extent, and in what ways, do perceptions construe and therefore affect the legitimacy of women's claims? To what extent does the existence of a legal 'right' signify existent perceptions of legitimacy? In what ways may the legitimacy of legal rights and therefore its effectiveness, be contingent upon the prior existence of perceptions of legitimacy? *Do these factors impact upon the legitimacy of women's claim to land as perceived by the women themselves? In particular,* what are their perceptions of self-interest and work contribution, *and how do these, if at all, in turn affect women's notions of legitimacy of land ownership through inheritance?*

Focusing upon individual Hindu small peasant women, the following analysis begins with the questions 'who is the individual woman that the law addresses the right to inherit to?' and 'within what constructions does she exist, if at all?' It became necessary to both explore the constructed identities, and search for aspects of identity outside the constructions. I use the term 'individual' to explore both these respects (Moore, 1995). Within the specific context of inheritance under the HSA, this duality presents a dichotomy. While the subject is taken as constituted by a specific relation as a member of the family and therefore subject to constructions by the ideology and power relations within it, she is simultaneously constituted as a holder of rights that are contrary to, and militate against, fundamental aspects of that ideology. It therefore becomes necessary to draw upon what women understood and perceived, to explore the dichotomy presented by law on the issue of the subjective identity of 'Hindu' women, necessarily through the expressions of the women themselves.[5]

Perception of 'Self-interest'

The most consistent response to the questions of individual self-interest posed before the women was one of non-comprehension and puzzlement. In fact, it was difficult to convey the idea of the self and self-interest to the women interviewed. Within the local dialect 'Sambalpuri', there is no word which may in definition be the corresponding word or term for 'self/individual interest'. If 'self-interest' is defined as the need and requirements of the individual, the Sambalpuri translation '*Nijjaur*' would mean the interest of the person concerned *inclusive* of others with whom the person is concerned or related, in this case the family to which the woman belongs. If others are to be excluded from the scope, it must be done expressly and explicitly. This requires that the question be rephrased in syntax to imply that their interest is exclusive of the interest of the family, which of course changes the issue to a wholly new and different one, with negative connotations of selfishness.

When posed with the broad question whether they *desire* acquisitions for themselves personally, for example, it was easily acknowledged that they did desire so, although the desire was neither determinate nor concrete. The issue of being entitled to these acquisitions on the basis of an exclusive claim, however, led to extreme confusion. The common reply was, 'myself alone? ... how can I think of myself alone? ..., what is there to think for myself? ...'. It was difficult to convey this idea of exclusivity, even through the use of examples of problematic situations which an individual woman might have to face, such as being destitute. But even to these scenarios the response was, '... *but how can I have a problem for myself?*' However, some of the woman did concede that if they did not obey their husbands and sons there would be a problem!

For the purposes of this study, the most significant finding was the depth and clarity in women's belief that the desire and furtherance of their individual interest would go against the interest of the family. They were, to begin with, unable and unwilling to distinguish between their own individual interest and the interest of the family as a whole. Further, their personal interest was in the welfare and benefit of their family.

> No, we don't think for ourselves alone, separate from our family and children. We can never think of ourselves alone once we are married, and have a husband, his family, and our children. Whatever we do is only for them.

The unambiguity with which 'family' overrides 'individual' is clear from the following:

---

5   I have discussed the importance of 'grounding' legal pluralism through reflection upon women's experiences, expressed in their own terms, in Patel (2005) 'Women's Right to Property Under Hindu Law: Gendered Entitlements and Traditional Obligations', *Indian Socio-Legal Journal* (*Special Issue on Legal Pluralism in India*, XXXI (Special), 73–94.

… "Myself, alone? What is there to think for myself?" … "I do think for myself that I may have a problem but then the problem is of the family because the whole family is there and we all work together but it cannot be mine alone." … "No way, no way … there cannot be a problem for me alone. How can I have a problem for myself? How can I think of myself alone?" … "as long as I have sons and daughters I can never think of anything as mine alone" …. "If I don't listen to my husband and sons then I will have a problem." … "I will worry about what to eat, what to wear, and what to drink and how to survive. I would need food and clothes" … "of course I would like to have something … if you go somewhere, would you not like to have some money of your own? But what if you have nothing? … No, I don't have anything. No land or farm or people and if you don't have anything and you have a problem then you can very well hang yourself and die. With so many people that is exactly what is happening and so many women hang themselves or eat poison and kill themselves because they don't have anything to live by."

Does the context of being resource-poor, where women do not have ownership over movable and immovable property of any significant value affect notions of individual entitlement? The responses alert us to a possible link between family well-being and individual empowerment. It is poignant that the extent of their self-interest is at best survival, and even the requirements for this such as food, clothing and shelter seem to be too much to expect sometimes, and giving up on survival itself seems to be a feasible option. The persistent poverty in the rural areas means that the women seek greater satisfaction through the improvement of their families' economic situation and of their status within the family. They see themselves as one component of the family and the extended group related by birth and marriage. The concept of individuality, exclusive of these structures, seems alien to them.

The Experience of Gender

But men enjoy their position because they are men, and we are inferior because we are women. This is our tradition and our culture. No matter how much we work, we will always be in this position once we are married. This is the base reality, no matter how much you may try to analyse otherwise. A woman can never think of anything as hers alone as long as she has sons and daughters …. Women belong to their husbands and depend on them …. What do my parents have to do with me? As a *daughter* I am not their responsibility any more. My parents will not give me anything. … "There is the expectation that sons will look after the parents in old age. As regards the daughter, it will depend on the marital family and how she relates to them, but the parents can't depend on them." … "In the case of a daughter, the parents cannot expect her to support them in difficulty because she belongs to another family after marriage."

"We do not worry about our daughters once they are married." … "Once she is married we are no longer responsible for her … parents have less responsibility towards their daughters than their sons" … "On the rare occasion that we go to their (the parents') home, they will take care of our needs But that is all we can expect."

The sense of not being part of the parents' family is deep-rooted. Marriage is the watershed in their lives when their ties with the natal family are severed, both socially and formally.

Even though sons and daughters might be equal so long as they are at home it changes after marriage .... Even if the girl were to live in the same village after marriage, it would be the same. Marriage itself means that the girl belongs to another family no matter where she lives. She is no longer part of the family.

When we get married, our ties are completely severed. We no longer have any right to expect anything in our parents home. In some communities they "immerse the bones" when a girl gets married. From then on, her life is in her husband's home, and it is here that she must find the means for survival.

(The reference is to the practice amongst Hindus of 'immersing' a deceased person's bones in the river or sea after cremation, in this case symbolizing the death of the daughter for her natal family.)

Although the lack of belonging in the parents home is justified by the idea that she will become part of her husband's family, which is a woman's real family, the reality is that even here women live in fear of being cast out. She belongs to the family, in the sense that it is at their pleasure that she enjoys the security of a home, but the home does not belong to her in any permanent secure way. The sense of insecurity is clearly experienced:

... so if I were to express any dissatisfaction at my situation, they (my husband and sons) will throw me out. That is so common .... Then where do I go? That is the difference between men and women that they can threaten to throw us out, but the sae thing does not apply to women. Because when the parents marry us off they have given us to the in-laws, and if they throw us out then where do we go? Men have a right in the house.

The insecurity felt by women reinforces, and in turn is reinforced by, the almost total dependence of the woman on her marital family after marriage. Together, the feelings of insecurity and dependence combine towards a position of fear, resignation and finally adaptation and co-optation within the dominant and patriarchal family structure, so the balance is maintained and their security is assured. The obligatory allegiance to the husband and his family is rationalized as necessitated by the need to maintain their material and emotional security:

"Her husband and his family will be responsible for her well-being" .... "Once we come to our in-laws after marriage, we have to *accept* whatever is our lot. It is the men who have the rights, so even if they were to commit the gravest wrongs they can never be wrong and no matter how much we do, we can never be right. And even if we were to make the smallest of mistakes, we would be ostracised."

"It is because of our tradition ... so if I acted according to what I thought my in-laws would not trust me any more, because they would think I am acting selfishly, and separating myself from the common objectives of the family" .... "After marriage, there is no choice, we have to work whether we want to or not. It is our duty"....

"As women, our honour lies in remaining within the house unless absolutely necessary and looking after the family interest therein, and in being obedient to our husbands. If we were to become the subjects of public discussions we will lose our honour, and thereby what is most important to us. The fear of this happening would stop us from doing anything that would, even remotely, cause such a loss of honour. No matter how desperate our situation we will protect our honour." "As far as property is concerned we will take the assistance from our brothers, husbands or parents. But we would not under any circumstances claim our share in the property."

Gender roles within society have been cast in specific and exclusive compartments such that the societal requirement of honour has been deeply embedded in women's psyche, ranking it above their physical well-being. On the other hand, it is the male role to provide and protect and it is expected and sanctioned for sons to support their parents. Further, the preference for sons is justified on religious grounds and in particular, upon the practice of offering oblations for the spiritual benefit of ancestors, and performing the funeral last rites of the parents. These, according to Hindu belief, shall be performed by the son and not the daughter.

As parents, we should treat both sons and daughters equally. But in our society, the way things are understood, we need sons. We need them for the offering of "pindas"[6] … whether one believes in it or not, one needs at least one son to offer "pindas" after one's death …. It is the tradition.

Women's roles and functions within the family and society provide the base upon which perceptions, values and ideas and identities are forged. How do these norms and values, the alienation of the girl from her natal family, and subsequent need to find security within the marital family, combine with these deeply imbibed ideas of the role of a female to affect the development of her personality, and her interpretation of the society around her? How does she then locate herself within the larger society and its institutions such as the law? These are issues that must be probed.

Right to Ownership of Land

The distinct correlation made between gender and ownership of land, as very succinctly pointed out, was that

The land goes to the men simply because they are men. It has nothing to do with who works on it. Whether the son wants to cultivate the land or leave it fallow, he will still have the right over that land.

In the words of another,

No, even if it was the practice for daughters to support parents in old age parents, it would make no difference to the daughter as far as the property is concerned, because no matter how much they acknowledge the daughter/sister's support, parents will never be willing to give land to daughters or sisters. Perhaps they will give her a tiny share, in memory of the father or the mother, but never more.

---

6   Offerings, made of rice balls, during the funeral rites of parents according to Hindu practice.

The sense of futility regarding the extent to which this ideology binds expresses itself in the denial of women's entitlement to a share even if they supported their parents:

> It would be futile, for no matter how much one does, for as long as there is a son, parents will never give their land to a daughter.

On the other hand, the same ideology became relevant in denying land to daughters and legitimizing such action as parents:

> "Parents do wish to provide for their daughters as well, but they are afraid of their son's reactions.' ... "How can we give them if there are sons? If we give her land when there is so little, what will we give to the sons?" ... "Daughters don't have as much right as a son in the father's land ... it's not the same as for sons". "There is the expectation that sons will look after the parents in old age, as regards the daughter it will depend on the marital family and how she relates to them, but they can't depend upon her support. How can she then in that case claim a right in the parents property. No matter how little the son has the parents would expect him to support him even by selling the last bit of land if need be. in case of a daughter after marriage she belongs to another family. so the parents cannot expect the same of her. Therefore we would not give land to a daughter."

The understandings of themselves as women – the specificities of their position within the family and society, their interaction with social and cultural norms and values as they perceive them, the absence of an interest exclusive to their individual selves, and the bias in favour of males – are all factors which combine to produce a particular conception of the right to ownership of land, which expressly includes only males and reinforces the exclusion of females.

> "I alone can't have a right" .... "Yes he (referring to the husband) has all the rights over it and can therefore do what ever he wants to do with the land. We (the wife and children) all have a right but he has more of a right. It is because the land belongs to him and because we depend on him and therefore also acquire a right over the land. It is because we belong to him that we are entitled to the property which is his". "Even if we were to be given land, we would not have the courage to assert ourselves."

The insecurity faced by women in the marital home imparts a particular significance upon their relations with the father and brothers. They depend upon them for support in case of trouble in the marital home. To this end, they use their share in the father's land as the means to ensure and maintain cordial relations with the natal family. The implicit understanding is that they will receive support from the brothers in troubled times, in return for relinquishing any claim over a share of the land. In this regard brothers hold a special place in a woman's life, paradoxically, after her marriage, when she is no longer part of her natal family.

> "How many would be willing to fight with their brothers. If it was convenient we would all claim our rights or shares." ... "Parents' property belongs to every body in the family. Where there is a good relation between the brothers and sisters perhaps it is possible. But otherwise it would be very difficult. Also it may be easy where there are only one son and daughter but in a situation there are more children particularly more brothers it is

impossible to think of the brothers giving up part of their already divided shares to their sisters. It does not happen like that" .... "That is why they do not claim, because brothers will turn against them. That is what will happen. Will women take the land and accept that they cannot go to the mother's house any more? Will they stop relating to everybody in the mother's family?"

Similarly, the relationship with the sons is based upon dependence in old age, and the necessity not to antagonize him by dividing his share with the sisters. Apart from the expectation that it is sons who will support the old parents, women face another issue – the possibility of widowhood. In this context, although they might in reality be legal owners of a share of the late husband's land, they are keenly aware of their physical dependence upon the son. Alone, without the husband, and possibly old themselves, they would not be able to either cultivate the land without the son's support, nor to be physically secure and cared for. This creates the need, therefore, to keep the sons happy, and not antagonize them, least of all by claiming their share in the husband's land, or lessening his share by giving the daughter her due.

" ... at least in theory we believe that we should have right over the land but in reality whether we would actually fight our sons is doubtful" .... "Where the sons are grown up or adults they can refuse to maintain us or give us any right in the family land. But we cannot do the same to them. From what the law is we should claim our shares but in reality we cannot."

Significantly, the issue of ownership was compounded where the property in question is land.

"It would be possible to claim if it were something else. Land is different.".... "It will not be given to us because it is fixed, and the income is continuous. In the case of jewellery, for example, no matter how much it is worth, it can only be sold once, and the income eventually exhausted. But in the case of land, the income is assured for always, however small. It is the source of income." ... "No, no matter what, land cannot be given." ... "In case of difficulty faced by the daughter, those who are in a position to do so will help their daughter or sister financially". "Where the subject is land, it can never be that no one else has any control over it simply because it belongs to me." ... "I would cause a separation between my husband and myself by referring to anything, most of all land, as mine."

Perspectives on Work and Contributions

I wake up around 4 in the morning, cleaning up after the previous day, cook the meal for the day, get the children ready for school and then leave for the field, around 8 in the morning. I return home around 1 p.m. By this time the children are also back from the school. After lunch, and a brief rest, I start the rest of the day's work at home, such as cooking, cleaning. I go to sleep around 10 p.m.

It is very clear that on the whole, taking into account both field as well as housework, there was no doubt that they, the women, worked more than the men of the household and that they were the primary workers in their families:

As far as work is concerned, women work more, because they not only work on the fields, but also in the house and look after the family in general.

In fact, it is the women who work more, even on the fields, in the various stages of cultivation throughout the year, until the crop is finally sold or ready for consumption.

However, the issue that was problematic was the recognition of their work by others; their family and the society. Though it was felt that their position was the same as their husbands and sons in terms of the work put in for the family, it was also felt that this was not how it was in fact perceived by their husbands and sons. As they perceived it, their work was not recognized and was considered to be useless in the society, even though they thought otherwise:

> Even if I work for eight days a week it is nothing, and if they (the men) do a little bit of work it is a lot. The way things are, I cannot say we should do this or that with the land, they are the ones who decide, and the women are supposed to be working as labourers as long as they have husbands and sons. As long as we have husbands and sons, we can only work for them .... Even if we work, it is not considered to be work.

Women's land ownership is related to the recognition of their work in a crucial way. Without ownership over the land they worked on, they became reduced to labourers, albeit unpaid ones; and the men, by virtue of ownership of the land in fact became the virtual owners of the women's work itself. The right of ownership also gives the man the greater power to decide on the use of the land.

> Another factor is that men in peasant households start believing that they have power over the work done by the women, because they are the owners of the land, that the women are working for them. So they will never acknowledge or recognise the women's work, or give her any freedom or right in recognition for the work done by them. Women therefore cannot decide on any issues relating to the work done on the land or otherwise for the sustenance of the family; at best they may only make suggestions which may or may not be accepted by the men.

Again, women's work is undervalued because it is considered to be part of their obligatory role in the marital household:

> The work we did at home was of our own free will, because we wanted to. After marriage, there is no choice, we have to work whether we want to or not. It is our duty .... In our cases at least, though women work much more than men, men enjoy a better position because they are men. They have a higher position because they are men, and we have an inferior position because we are women. No matter how much we work, we will always be in this position once we are married. This is the reality, this is in our culture and tradition.

Further, the practice of seclusion which inculcates the feeling of 'shame', arising from the fact that women are the upholders of honour and respect of the family to the world at large, also plays a role. Women feel restricted in contesting these attitudes towards their work, for to do so would bring the matter into the public domain, and make them subject to the public gaze, thereby derogating from their honour and causing them and their families shame:

> In the middle classes, as opposed to the lowest classes of peasant women, the women are restrained because of the feeling of shame which they have. So in the case of women like us, we would be much more reluctant to make public in any manner an issue that is related to our home. This is both because of the feeling of shame and our fear of society.

In the Context of Labourers

The position of women labourers was perceived by the non-wage earning cultivators to be better than their own as regards recognition of work and position in the family. Women labourers were perceived to have more authority in the household owing to the fact that they earned their own money.

> And where both of them are working on others' land, the men cannot dominate the women as much as our men do. After all, both of them are working, and he knows that, so what can he say to dominate them?... In the labourer's family, both of them earn money, and with that money buy food for sustenance. For women who are small peasants and work to grow their own food, it is more difficult to get their work recognised ... that is why many women who are small peasants think it is better if they were to become labourers, so that they would at least get paid for the work done.

Women who worked as wage labourers were perceived to not have the same constraints of social sanction through 'shame' and honour as women working on their family land:

> In the middle income families as opposed to the low classes of women, the women are restrained because of the feeling of shame which they feel with respect to men. On the other hand low class women do not have the same restricting factors. So in the case of women like ours we would be much more reluctant to make public in any manner an issue which is related to our home. This is both because of the feeling of shame and the fear of the society.

Work and Ownership of Land – Is there a Connection?

There are three issues here: First, is there a desire for some return for the work done by the women? Secondly, what is the return/reward as they perceive it? And third, can ownership of land be a return for work done? Notwithstanding the expectation of some material returns for the work done, it is conceived only as the means to their survival, in terms of food, clothing and shelter, and totally excludes land. Asked if there is anything more that they perceive as a reward for work done, the answer was, the welfare of the family. All of them identified this as their reward, and were horrified at the suggestion that perhaps they should want something more:

> "We get nothing except the satisfaction that we are doing something for the family." ...
> "No, we do not think in terms of returns for our work in that sense. We think that we work

for the welfare of the family, and not in terms of our personal efforts and rewards. So, the satisfaction, however little, that our children and family are being looked after is our reward. We cannot expect anything more."

"We do not get anything apart from our means of survival, and the satisfaction that the children and family are being looked after, with the expectation that we will have the security of being looked after when we ourselves grow old .... No, we don't think of ourselves alone, separate from our family and children. We can never think for ourselves once we are married. Whatever we do is only for the children, husband, in-laws." ... "Nothing can be ours alone. Whatever we earn belongs to everyone in the family. If I were to say anything is mine, everyone else is equally likely to do the same." "How can we think of being compensated for what we do for our home? When we have given birth to children, we have to look after them. It is our responsibility. They will grow up well only if we devote ourselves to them, and not if we are trying to separate what is ours as opposed to theirs." "We don't think we should have a right in the property. If they give us a share, fine, if they don't, even that's fine. In this family, everything is ours after all − the mother-in-law, the father-in-law, the husband, the children. So what is there to separate as mine after that?"

Conclusion: Can the Right to Own Land Be a Reward for Work Done?

"We do think of a reward, but not in terms of getting our individual share of land .... There is no correlation, in our mind, between our work, and the fact that we don't own property. If tomorrow we were to be totally excluded from the land, we would stay away .... There is no relation of work with who owns property." "The land goes to men simply because they are men. It has nothing to do with who works on it. Whether the son wants to cultivate it or leave it fallow, he will still have *a* right to the land." "If the brothers do not look after us, our parents cease to care for us, only then would we think of a share in land."

The limited resources available to these groups of peasants is significant towards rejecting the idea of individual claims.

"When there is barely enough for the family's needs, how can we think of our own share." ... "As it is, there is so little. There is one plough, a tiny bit of land. My brothers have to survive on that. How can I then think of a share in that as mine, and still expect to be cared for by them?"

To conclude, the operation of gender biased ideology locates the women of my sample within a matrix where the individual self is minimized. Simplistically, how does this bode for the operation of law especially property law, which starts with a presumption of the clarity of individual wants/needs/desires? The only aspect where the individual in the woman is recognized and understood as such is the recognition of themselves as workers. Beyond that, the individual needs and desires extend to include the family.

The perceptions of women, that they are not entitled to a share in parental property, were clearly expressed. The knowledge of their formal rights to acquire a share does not in any way impact upon the fact that their lives, entitlements and rights are informed by very different norms and world views. Formal laws do not appear to form part of this discourse.

This discussion highlights the construction of Hindu peasant women's claim to land derived from religious ideology. In particular, it highlights the role of 'Hindu' women within the family, and the operation of religious ideology to construct the 'Hindu' female as essentially precluded from independent property ownership. The near-impossibility of claiming ownership of family land through succession for most of the women arises out of their perceptions and understandings of themselves as Hindu women, of their role and position within their families, and the operation of religious ideology to inform these. Whereas they do not have an interest in claiming land through succession, the religion-derived gender ideology precludes, as Hindu women, from substantiating their right to succession as Hindu women. Although the discussions show that their experiences as peasant women engaged in work and production provide the basis for their interest in land ownership at least in some contexts, it remains limited to the extent that religious and gender ideology combine to devalue their work and contribution. A significant point, however, is that this devaluation, is not subscribed to by the women themselves, but understood as ascribed by religious ideology. This provides an instance where the dichotomy is collapsed; where as Hindu women, they express their claim (within the family/household) as a result of their work and contribution as peasants in agricultural production.

What then, is the content/ideology of the law, supposedly formulated to 'empower' women and bring about social change? Why is it invisible in these women's lives and insignificant in affecting the norms they are bound by? The succeeding chapters will discuss this.

Chapter 5

An Evaluation of Women's Self-Interest in the Hindu Law of Succession

Introduction

As we have seen previously, the HSA lays out the framework within which Hindu women's claim to land is constructed. This construction is addressed to Hindu women, where the claim is to property within the family through succession. In this chapter, the specific contours of this construction within law and its effect upon Hindu women's claim to land are examined. In order to evaluate women's ability to own land independently, conceptualizing women's access to land as an aspect of bargaining allows us to analyse both internal factors such as ideological persuasions, as well as external factors such as their role in work and contribution. Having established the HSA as constitutive of the ideological framework of law, this chapter will address the issue of how this ideological framework operates to affect Hindu women's claim to land constituted within HSA.

I discuss the impact of the ideology implicit within HSA upon Hindu women's self-interest to land – the 'internal' aspect which affects the bargaining position and ultimately their claim to land. In this chapter, we draw out certain concepts and parameters of women's self-interest underlying and pervasive within Hindu law, and the extent to which this does or does not strengthen Hindu women's ability to contest for land through succession. The extent to which the legal provisions, notwithstanding the introduction of values with the aim of enabling women's equal position, in fact continue to promote the pre-existing values which disentitled women will be scrutinized. In doing so, examples will be drawn from case law and judicial decisions. Decisions by courts are here used to reflect upon the depth of underlying values regarding the female in Hindu Law. To the extent that these are reiterated in cases by judges, values antithetical to women's independent status and ownership rights continue to be enforced and emphasized within judgements as normative rules having the sanction of law. In particular, it will be shown that women's interest to acquire property independently, through succession, promoted on the one had by the provisions of statutory laws, is in fact overshadowed by law's stronger promotion of women's interest as engulfed within that of the family, and the non-recognition of their individual interest, separate from their family.

With the background information regarding women's successory rights within the contemporary Hindu law in Chapter 3, we can begin to draw out specific aspects of values and principles affecting women embodied within Hindu law. Statements, arguably having the force of prescription regarding, women's position and roles contained in Hindu religious texts which formed the 'Shastric' basis of Hindu law will be shown to be very much operative as principles of Hindu law through the reference to selected judicial decisions in post-independence India. Further, these aspects will also be shown to be reflective of perceptions and understandings of women's role and identity as expressed by women in the field, brought out in Chapter 4.

A discussion of key aspects of the identity of Hindu women will complete the analysis of the effect of law's sanction of the roles idealized by religion and culture. The roles, values and position accorded to Hindu women, sanctioned and upheld by the legal framework ultimately have the effect of constituting, and to the extent that law is aimed at changing, in fact perpetuating, Hindu women as persons whose interest is completely submerged with that of the family. While women identify themselves more with the family of the husband, the legal changes assume and take into account her identity with the natal family. Further, this assumption is extended to include the ability of women, as daughters, to compete with brothers within the same family for the fulfilment of their interest to independent ownership of land in the natal family within which their identity is assumed.

Resonance of Contemporary Perceptions with Models from the Past

Ancient Hindu literature provides us with a rich source of details, statements, prescriptions and canons regarding the position, role and nature of a female. While many may be seen to be purely textual works and regarded for their skill of representation and language as literary works alone, Hindu tradition is based upon textual works to a significant extent. The *Smritis* and within them the *Shastras* form a substantial basis of values and principles guiding religious and spiritual practice over millennia (Madan, 1979). The interactions between some aspects of Hindu philosophy, mythology, worship and morality combine to create a way of life that is neither a religion nor a philosophy alone, but nevertheless constitute for the Hindu a set of distinct principles and values. Women's roles, behaviour and morality are the subject of a rich base of narratives through mythology, stories and characters which have served to crystallize themes and ideals. The characters of Sita, Savitri and Sati are but few of numerous revered household names, each embodying ideals of womanhood.

The particular development and role of Hindu textual works in Indian society has been shaped by its colonial history. Alongside the 'institutionalisation' of legal rules during colonial rule as discussed in Chapter 2, this process of colonial engagement also shaped and concretized the content of Hindu 'tradition' through the greater generation of publications, local literature and public debate. The orientalist engagement with 'Hindu' society as the subject of colonial rule produced two, apparently conflicting but mutually reinforcing currents. On the one hand, it invigorated the publication and narrative of 'Hindu' custom, practice and values at the local and regional levels. However, at the same time it necessitated a wider process of selection, definition and attempted homogenization of 'Hindu' society. Sangari (1999) critically analyses the process of an evolving narrative on gender within the politics of colonial engagement. Commenting on the depth and extent of prescriptions and proscriptions shaping this narrative, she notes:

The "thickness" of detail of patriarchal ideologies from different times and spaces is not a product of ethnographic ambition or the literary habit of careful reading. Rather, it both reproduces my own shock of familiarity and is a subterranean articulation of the complex itinerary of prescriptive texts across regions and historical periods, the transnational (re)formation, the long duration and resilience of patriarchies as a consequence of their conjugation with other systemic forms of oppression (1999: xivi).

From the plethora of stories, epics and myths which served as tales of normativity for women and continue to do so today, this chapter draws upon statements in the *Manusmriti* as a guide to understanding and critically evaluating the same. Although it is undoubtedly correct that the *Manusmriti* cannot be held up as 'the' lawbook of the Hindus as it is often mistakenly claimed to be,[1] it is nevertheless important to note the importance of this text as a primary instrument for the attempted progressive homogenization of Hindu society. Within this, it is also a significant text as embodying various normative codes for the appropriate behaviour of women. As Sangari notes,

A product of early class stratification, compressing domestic, ritual and reproductive labour into salvation for women, debarring them from most religious activities, instituting controls at a time when practices were probably more flexible, the Manusmriti was later selectively universalized for castes and regions beyond its own intentionality and historical spread .... Not surprisingly, then, it became an Ur-text invoked by ideologically disparate reformers ... throughout the colonial period (1999: 315).

Thus, many of the injunctions and dicta which attributed to and contained in the *Manusmriti* with regard to the role, nature and position of females in Hindu society, are echoed in other texts by other writers and over different periods (Leslie, 1995; Sangari, 1999).[2] Further, the *Manusmriti* has the position, effectively, of the most authoritative reservoir of Hindu law; due both to its traditional history and the systematic and cogent collection of existing rules that it sets out and the largest number of commentaries (Madan, 1979; Mulla, 1990). It gives a vivid idea of society and customs within the 'Hindu' fold as it has been continuously elaborated upon and reproduced through history and contemporary periods. It must be clear, however, that the *Manusmriti* is used here only as an example of the textual source of obligations and codes addressed to Hindus. The point is important to note, that the references drawn from the text in this chapter serve two functions: as symbolic of the tenor of social/normative prescriptions towards women and illustrative of a range of narratives dealing with similar subjects/themes. Further, that the scope of the *Manusmriti* extends to a vastly greater number of subjects than dealt with here, hence references contained in this may not be held to be misrepresentative. My references to it will be drawn from commentaries and translations by other historians and authors.

---

1   For a thorough discussion of the incorrectness of dealing with *Manusmriti* in this fashion, see further, Menski (2003), particularly the Introduction.

2   For a thorough and critical analysis of the continued reliance on the Manusmriti in more accessible and popular forms and texts well into the twentieth century, see particularly Sangari (1999).

Together with the a drawing out of principles relating to women's lives within the Hindu socio-religious framework as illustrated by writings within these texts, this chapter incorporates their application within the legal framework, where they have been expounded and applied, by reference to judicial decisions in the field of Hindu law. As noted in the previous section, Hindu law today is comprised of a plurality of norms derived from a variety of sources. However, the point to be reiterated, drawing from the outline in the preceding section, is the centre stage given to a religious perspective in the evolution of Hindu law. What this denotes is twofold: first, that although statutory and judicial developments have sought to introduce hitherto alien principles within Hindu law, they are at the same time *bounded* by and draw validity from the broader framework of Hindu law and second, that the ideas, principles and resulting norms contained within what may otherwise be considered to be purely religious texts are transformed into binding principles of law. While this falls within the Hindu conception of law that law is an expression of *Dharma*, in the context of post-independence developments through statutory law this in fact becomes a limiting principle for the purposes of introducing new principles within this framework, particularly if these are in conflict with religious prescription.

The particular aspects regarding the position of females in the family and wider society as prescribed under traditional Hindu law discussed here are: (a) position of female as wife, daughter and widow (b) significance of marriage (c) duties and Obligations (e) the right of women to hold property and (f) the concept of *Stridhana*.

Position of Female as Daughter, Wife and Widow

The Daughter

From ancient times, Hindu society has preferred the birth of a son to a daughter. The gods are invoked through hymns, to grant sons to the bride. Indeed, daughters are conspicuous in the Rig-Veda by their absence (Das, 1993). In later periods of history too male progeny continued to be distinctly preferred to female ones. The daughter is declared to be a source of misery while the son is the saviour of the family, the latter is the only hope of the family, while the former is a source of trouble to it. Many hymns, especially within the marriage ceremony, express the preference for a male offspring, such as in the *Saptapadi*,[3] where the bridegroom addresses the bride as follows:

> Come now, let us beget, let us place the seed together that we may attain a male child (Mitter, 1984, 198).

During the marriage ceremony, the prayer of the bridegroom is to Indra,[4] to grant his bride 10 sons. Ceremonies such as the *Garbhadhana*[5] ceremonies reveal the keen

---

3 Part of the marriage ceremony where the bride and the groom take seven steps in front of the ritual fire.

4 Indra is the King of the gods in the Hindu pantheon.

5 *Garbadhana* was a ceremony to mark the conception of a child by a married woman, and to offer prayers for the well-being of both mother and child.

desire of ancient Aryans to have a male offspring, and medicinal herbs were given to the pregnant woman in order to conceive a male child. The same anxiety for the securing of a male child is reflected in the act of placing a male child in the lap of the bride when she arrives at her husband's home after the marriage. The anxiety of begetting a male child is reflected by special ceremonies, as well as the prayers offered in others for the purpose. The prayer is, 'The birth of a girl, grant it elsewhere, here grant a son'. It is further prayed that the male children be followed by male offspring only and never by female ones.

The birth of a female child did not cause much rejoicing, and she was put aside as the male child was received by the parents with joy. The grounds for preferring a son to a daughter were that the son always remained with the parents, continued the family line, offered oblations to the ancestors for the spiritual benefits, was a support to the parents in their old age and helplessness and added lustre and glory to the good name of the family by his noble and brilliant achievements (Das, 1993). That this preference is very much alive and given legitimacy in contemporary society is proved by judicial pronouncements making reference to the son's duties to maintain the parent and thereby entitled to the property on this basis. Although the case of Sushila Bala Saha[6] was one where the court in fact upheld the disinheritance of the son in favour of a daughter, it highlights the norm; that the basis of entitlement to property is a gendered one, where the primary entitlement is that of a son. However, the case also sets the boundaries for such entitlement, as based upon the obligation to support. In this, it opens up the possibility of change and the entitlement of the daughter within these boundaries.

As for the daughter, she was considered more a liability than an asset. There was a change in her *gotra*[7] after her marriage (Mitter, 1984), upon marriage she migrated to another family and therefore ceased to have any direct spiritual benefit for her parents. Nevertheless, it was required of the father to maintain and educate his daughters, and to give them in marriage before they attained puberty to suitable bridegrooms. On the death of the father, the duty devolves upon the brother or the then head of the family, whoever he might be (Sen, 1984). She remained a burden as substantial amounts of money had to be spent on the occasion of her marriage and even if she were married, she had to be maintained in the case of the death of her husband or poverty.

In the event of her remaining unmarried she had to be provided for with the apportionment of a share in the family property and she also had to be guarded from going astray. The chastity of females had to be protected, it being the highest virtue of a maiden. The duty of the father to secure the marriage of his daughter, in addition to that of protecting his daughter's virtue placed him in the position of great moral responsibility. Failure to fulfil it merited sanction if, for example, a man failed to give his daughter in marriage before the start of her menstruation cycle. According to the Manusmriti, such a father loses dominion over his daughter, and any man who marries such a girl shall not pay anything to her father (Das, 1993).

---

6   *Sushila Bala Saha v Saraswati Mondal* AIR 1991 Cal 166.

7   *Gotra* is the group to which a person belongs, tracing descent from a common principal sage, and in the case of non-brahmins, adopting the *gotra* of the Brahmin priest.

Again, in a similar situation, a girl who was not married by her father at the right time becomes free to choose her own husband, although it was not encouraged in practice. Regarding a maiden's virtue, a father who had failed to protect his daughter's virginity is not liable to punishment if he discloses such 'liability' at her wedding (Das, 1993).

The duties of the father/male head of the family towards the daughter are corresponding to restraints placed upon the daughter. The very import and significance of these duties lie on the fact that they are postulated upon the total dependence of the female as wife, mother or daughter. *Manusmriti* declares that women are not expected to act independently as they like, whether they be girls, in youth, or old aged women, 'nothing should be done independently by a woman, either as a child, a young girl or old woman, even in her (own) home' (Leslie, 1995, 276). They are exhorted to obey the commands of the fathers during their childhood, their husbands during their youth, and their sons after the demise of their husbands and not depend on themselves (Subamma, 1992). The characterization of the daughter as a non-independent subject is also clear from the fact that the daughter was in fact treated as the property of her father until the age of marriage.

Within the context of the father's duty to secure his daughter's marriage, arose a multitude of rules governing the marriage of a daughter. For example, it was not in keeping with the grace and modesty expected of a daughter to choose her own husband, therefore she was discouraged from doing so even where the father was slow to discharge his duty of getting her married. The idealization of the daughter as a non-independent acting subject is again made clear by holding that form of marriage as the highest of the eight recognized forms, where the girl is a gift of the father, pure and simple.[8]

The result is the construction of a daughter's identity in terms of the father's duties towards her, premised upon the undesirability of her acting independently. Further, while such identity therefore takes account of her relations with her natal family, the focus upon her marriage and subsequent alienation from the natal family makes such relation by its nature, very tenuous. The result therefore, is an identity that is not secure or complete even in its definition by the factors that construct it. The temporary and transient nature of a daughter's membership within her maternal home as being a social fact, taken into account by contemporary Hindu law and to that extent reinforcing her position is reflected in the fact that in addition to the provisions of the HSA distinguishing between married and unmarried daughters, the Hindu Adoption and Maintenance Act 1956[9] includes the married and widowed daughter as dependants, but excludes the married daughter as liable to be maintained.

The Wife

The construction of the daughter, as a liability and with whom the parents' relation was to a great extent defined by their onerous responsibility to give her

---

8   The *Brahma* form of marriage, is a gift of the girl to a man learned in the Vedas.
9   Section 21.

in marriage, is the precursor of her role as a wife. It is upon becoming a wife that a female assumes her ideal role, where she may fulfil her obligations to her husband, his family and society, and thereby live a virtuous life. In the relation of the wife to the husband, his family and wider society, it is possible to draw out three predominant aspects: the requirement of chastity, the predominance of duties and obligations in her relationship with her husband and extending to his family and the possibility of sanction through supercession for non-fulfilment of her obligations.

Chastity The chastity of the wife was of paramount significance, for according to the Manusmriti,

> One must guard the wife against sensual contact, as the ruin of the wife involves the ruin of the family, ruin of the family involves the ruin of the line, the ruin of offerings involve the ruin of the soul, and ruin of the soul means the ruin of all things (Das, 1993, 81).

However, the defects inherent in the nature of women, that

> "Women do not dwell on beauty nor is their attention fixed on age; simply for the fact that he is a man, they give themselves to the handsome and the ugly. Through their natural heartlessness, they become disloyal to their husband, howsoever carefully they may be guarded in this world". These defects are inherent in their nature; for Manu says, "When creating them, the creator allotted to women a love of bed, of their seat of ornaments, impure desires, wrath, dishonesty, malice and bad conduct" (Sen, 1984, 227).

required that chastity had to be guarded by the husband:

> Women must particularly be guarded against evil inclinations, however trifling they may appear to be; for if they are not guarded, they will bring sorrow to both the families. Considering it the highest duty of all castes, even weak husbands must strive to guard their wives .... He who carefully guards his wife preserves the purity of his offspring, virtuous conduct, his family, himself and his means of acquiring merit (Das, 1993, 81).

These comments have contemporary resonance, echoed in the comment by Sen (1984) that the protection of women is necessary, for they are by nature weak and unable to bear the turmoil of the world and stand against its terrors and temptations without guidance and control.

But this guarding is not to be done by force. It is not possible for husbands to guard their wives by force. The Manusmriti suggests three ways of doing this. Firstly, the importance of chastity must be inculcated in their mind so that they might themselves be their own guards. Secondly, they should be kept away from drinking, associating with wicked people, tendency to keep away from the husband rambling, sleeping and residing at other peoples houses, because these things help to corrupt the mind of the women and they come to lose all fear of their father-in-law and others as also the regard for public opinion. Thirdly, the husband should try to keep her engaged in the management of the household affairs so that she may not have an idle moment to think or do any undesirable or shameful acts.

Let the husband employ his wife in the collection and expenditure of his wealth, in keeping everything clean, in the fulfilment of the religious duties, in the preparation of the food and in the looking after the household-utensils (Das, 1993, 82).

The requirement for chastity is significant in any analysis of the position of a Hindu wife. While it is correct to note that the basic right of the wife to be maintained by her husband persists notwithstanding her unchastity, the pervasiveness of the religious prescriptions as normative and binding principles to be taken into account by law is evident from the implications of unchastity in contemporary law. The Hindu Adoptions and Maintenance Act, 1956[10] nullifies the right of a Hindu wife to claim maintenance if she is unchaste, even if she may be living apart from her husband under any of the grounds recognized by the Act.

Duties and obligations   Starting with the principle that she is never to act independently, the foremost duty of the wife was to serve, obey and honour her husband, for it is her husband who gives pleasure to the wife in both the worlds (Sharma, 1990).

Him, to whom her father may give her or her brother with the father's permission, she shall obey as long as he lives and when he is dead she must not insult his memory. A faithful wife who wishes to dwell in this as well as the next world must never do anything that might displease him who took her hand, whether he is alive or dead (Das, 1993, 75).

A chaste wife must adore and worship him as god even if the husband is addicted to bad ways or debauchery, or lacks good qualities. Only by serving her husband can she attain an honourable place in heaven; the wife is not entitled to perform sacrifices, undertake fasts or other forms of worship for herself (Subamma, 1992).

Even though destitute of virtue or seeking pleasure elsewhere or devoid of good qualities, yet a husband must be constantly worshipped as a god by a faithful wife. No sacrifice, no vow, no fast must be performed by the wife apart from her husband; if a wife serves her husband, she will, for that reason alone be exalted in heaven (Das 1993, 74).

Thus, the only means of salvation for a wife was in the unquestioning, complete service towards her husband.

Moreover, a wife should not seek to become independent. In her youth she must not seek to separate herself from her husband, she must be under his control. By leaving him she, would make both her own and his family despised in the society. When the husband is no more, her husband's relations would protect her; in their absence some one of her father's side shall be her protector and on the total extinction of both the families the king shall be her guardian (Das, 1993).

In the course of everyday life, the specific duties of the wife included the duty to look after the household work. She was to manage the household in consultation with her husband on the general principle above, that by a woman nothing must be done independently, even in the household. She must be talented in doing household work, keep the household articles clean and shall keep away from wasteful habits:

---

10 Section 18(3).

She must always be clever in the management of the household affairs, careful in cleaning the utensils and economical in expenditures (Subamma, 1992, 65).

She is further required to avoid drinking spirituous liquor, associating with wicked people, separation from the husband, rambling about, sleeping at unusual hours, dwelling in others houses. These are also the reasons for the ruin of the woman, contaminating the mind of the woman, and they come to lose all the fears of their father-in-law and others and also regard for the public opinion. The result is that they are easily led astray into the evil ways of life.

The duties of the wife towards her husband are a derivative of the primary rule that a wife must live with her husband. This plays a very significant role in various issues within Hindu law, such as restitution of conjugal rights, grounds for judicial separation and claims for maintenance by the wife in any circumstance, as traditionally the right to maintenance is based upon her residence with the husband. However, within such residence, the rules for the conduct of the wife within marriage and her duty of obedience and service to the husband also have a significant bearing upon her claim to maintenance. The court, while determining the amount of a claim for permanent alimony and maintenance under Section 25 of the Hindu Marriage Act, may take into account, among others, the conduct of the parties.

Supercession The Manusmriti provides that in certain cases the wife may be deprived of her conjugal rights which were transferred to another wife taken by the man later on; for the forsaking of one wife and taking another. The conduct expected of the wife described above assumes the nature of binding obligations, upheld by sanction. While the specific directions regarding chastity or duties towards the husband are based upon the ideals of fulfilment in the next life, supercession presents a threat of an outcome in this life itself. The moral code, premised upon one's existence in the next life, is thus translated into a socially binding code, addressed to one's position in this society and world.

Supercession could not be possible so long as the wife was virtuous and was endowed with offspring. If, however she was wanting in these two things, the man could take another wife. If the wife failed in her duties towards her husband and her family or failed to be virtuous in her conduct and dealings with them, she was liable to be superseded. The Manusmriti lays great emphasis on the fact that the wife should not be quarrelsome or even harsh in speech. If she is quarrelsome none of the duties of the married life could be properly performed nor the pleasures of life be enjoyed in her company. Further, such behaviour on the part of the wife would result in the loss of peace in the family. Therefore, a sharp-tongued wife, speaking unpleasant things was to be immediately superseded.

> She, who drinks spirituous liquor, is of bad conduct, rebellious, diseased mischievous or wasteful, may at any time be superseded by another wife (Das, 1993, 85–95.)

Again, if a wife fails to bear sons, she could be superseded. However, if she was of a good nature and virtuous in her conduct, her consent could be sought for her supercession. Similarly, a barren wife also could be superseded.

Where a man justifiably decided upon the supercession of his wife, as in cases of her being of false conduct, diseased, mischievous, wasteful or habitual alcoholic, the wife does not have a choice but to accept her supercession. As a means of ensuring her acceptance the Manusmriti upholds:

> A wife, who being superseded, in anger departs from her husband's house must be instantly confined only for so long as she becomes free from anger and comes to her senses. But if it is not possible to control her through confinement, she is to be abandoned in the presence of the family (Das, 1993, 87).

She is to be 'abandoned' by her husband and his family, and in her maternal home, till her anger subsidies and she has regained the ability to live peacefully in her husbands home.

The Widow

Having traced the position of the female as a daughter and wife, it is clear that she in fact occupies a totally dependent position, first to her parents, and thereafter to her husband and his family. It is upon the condition of widowhood, however, that the full force of the notions previously fostered come into play. On the issue of family relations, the separation from her natal family, completed at her marriage, continues. At the same time, although she assumes membership of her husband's family, this is in fact never complete, and she continues to remain in many senses an outsider. The resulting fact is one of vulnerability and near-total alienation, where she can in fact no longer depend upon anyone, even though dependence is precisely the condition fostered in her from her earliest days. This isolation is in fact normalized in the writings of the Manusmriti. Self-denial and reclusivity become the ideals for widowhood:

> ... let her rather emaciate her body by living upon pure flowers, roots and fruits, but let her not, when her husband is dead, even to pronounce the name of another man, and longing for the unparalleled virtue of those who remain steadfast to one husband, let her lead a life of austerity, strictly observing the rules of continence and foregoing all sensual pleasures until she dies (Sen, 1984, 277).

In this context, the central issue regarding widows becomes the question of their remarriage, for it is through marriage that she may become part of society again. The duties of a wife within marriage as contained within the Manusmriti precludes her from remarrying. The Manusmriti contains opposition to widow remarriage, as is clear from the pronouncement that a second husband of a good woman is nowhere prescribed (Das, 1993). The practice of widow remarriage is further discouraged by the assertion that a woman who violates her duty to remain faithful to her deceased husband brings upon herself disgrace in this world and loses her place with her husband in heaven.

Apart from the spiritual downfall, the practice of preventing widow-remarriage was sanctioned and the son of a remarried widow was precluded from being treated as an heir to his father, even in the absence of a legitimate son. Such a son was only entitled to food and clothing. Most important of all, the father of such a son is also affected for he cannot derive any spiritual benefit from him (Das, 1993). If, however, she remains true to her duty to be faithful to her husband,

> On her husband's death if a virtuous woman abides by the rules of celibacy, she goes straight to heaven though she be sonless ... (Das, 1993, 110).

The reality of widowhood is in fact more heinous today than may be gleaned from what I have dealt with above. The practices and prejudices directed against widows once again are commonly drawn from a reading of religious texts and interpretations thereof. In short, the extreme isolation, rejection and vulnerability a widow faces is as great today, if not greater in many communities in India (Dreze and Sen, 1999).

This brings into focus another aspect that follows from the above. In enduring the difficulties of a life of widowhood, one of the mainstays of a woman's life becomes her relationship with her children, particularly the son (Mandelbaum, 1970). As brought out earlier, a widow is doubly alienated, from her parents, as well as in-laws. In such a situation, her reliance is largely upon her children, for she becomes dependent upon their support, physical, material and emotional. In particular, it is the son she relies upon, for as we have seen earlier, the daughter's residence is only temporary and the parents cannot have any legitimate expectations of her after her marriage. It is the son moreover, who has the spiritual obligation to maintain his parents in Hindu law, not the daughter. A widow who sought a share is described as weak and without support as

> ... an old lady in late sixties and literate, not well versed in the ways of the world ... leading the sheltered life of a widow in an orthodox family ... very much dependent ... on the brother of her late husband ... she had no sons or support to look to ....[11]

The Significance of Marriage

In considering the significance of marriage upon a woman in the philosophy of the Manusmriti and other Hindu codes, it would not be an exaggeration to say that her entire life revolved around it; further, that it is as a householder, within marriage, that she performs her greatest function, 'for women, the marriage ritual is held to be the equivalent of initiation, serving one's husband that of residing in the teacher's house, and household duties that of the worship of sacrificial fire' (Leslie, 1995, 35). The sacrament of marriage within Hindu law was founded upon the notion of a complete union of the spouses. However, the entry of the wife into this union is based upon her 'taking a new birth' as her husband's partner, and severing her membership with her maternal family to becoming a member of his family (Sharma, 1990).

Marriage is one of the four stages ordained in the life of a Hindu, namely, that of being a student, a householder, a hermit and finally, a renunciate. In the philosophy explicated within the Manusmriti the order of the householder, or *Grahasthashrama*, is the most important sacrament. The indispensability of marriage as an individual,

---

11 *A Venkappa Bhatta v Gangamma* AIR 1988 Kerala, 133.

social and religious necessity makes it a *saria samskara*, a refining process, through which every man and woman must pass at the proper age and time:

> As all living creatures subsist by receiving support from the air, so all Orders subsist by receiving support from the householder. Because the men of the three Orders are daily supported by the householder with sacred knowledge and food, therefore the householder's is the most excellent Order. The duties of this Order must be carefully observed by him who desires imperishable bliss in heaven and constant happiness in this life. The student, the householder, the hermit and the ascetic, these all spring from the Order of the householders. And in accordance with the Vedas the housekeeper is declared to be superior to all of them; for he supports all three. As all rivers, both great and small find a resting place in the ocean, even so men of all Orders find protection with the householder (Das, 1993, 42).

Thus, marriage, which gave rise to the household, was regarded as necessary and desirable for all. It was thought that marriage was a prime necessity, and it was marriage alone that could help a person discharge his religious and secular obligations (Mulla, 1990). Most significantly for a female, marriage is the only sacrament prescribed for her in Hindu law.

As pointed out earlier, the life of an unmarried daughter in her father's home is one of waiting, where she is but a temporary member. It is upon marriage that she is transplanted into her permanent home, that of her husband. This process is one whereby she must marry and sever ties with her parental home and as result is unable to maintain a continuing relationship as a daughter. To this end, the sacred obligation of the parents to give their daughter in marriage ensures the compliance by the parents and the completion of the cycle. A daughter, on her part accepts her eventual transferral to another family and the transience of her relations within her natal family and the parents, on their part, endure the pain of severance of the daughter's ties upon her marriage on account of their duty.

The most significant aspect of the sacramental nature of a Hindu marriage, as Derrett points out,

> … is not that the notion would stand in the way of nullity (often it would not), but it makes the wife a full member of her husband's family, related to his parents and siblings exactly as if she had been born in the family, and it is this which is indissoluble …. By contrast western marriages unite only the spouses and they can be, and not infrequently are, indifferent to the parents on both sides, let alone the sibling (Derrett, 1970, 160).

Within the marriage sacrament the daughter is 'given' by her father, and is only a passive party to the marriage. This is borne out by the fact that an essential part of the marriage ceremony entails '*Kanyadaan*' literally meaning, 'gift of the maiden'. As Mitter (1984) points out, under Hindu law, the man is the active and the woman the passive agent in the transaction, for a man is said to 'marry', whereas a woman is said to be 'given in marriage'. The doer of the act is the man, the act is the marriage, and the object of the act is the wife (Mitter, 1984).

The Hindu interpretation of marriage envisages it as a process whereby the woman is transferred as a gift from one household to another. She thereby acquires a new identity and status, and concomitant rights and responsibilities vis-à-vis her husband's kin, while relinquishing those in respect of her own kin. Where both husband and wife insisted on their obligation to stay with their family of origin, they were reminded:[12]

> Mrs Tewari and her mother must realise that *after marriage the wife's home is where the husband lives and the husband's family has to be considered by her to be her family. Her mother must grasp this vital fact, taking it for granted that after the marriage the girl has to go and live with her husband.* She must, therefore, adjust herself to the changed situation after her daughter's marriage. Similarly, Shri Tewari and his brother and mother have to face the new situation created by the marriage. The introduction of his wife in his family means that all the family members must welcome her with affection and they must help her in all respects to strengthen the roots in the family life of her husband. Mrs Tewari has to look upon her new mother-in-law as her own mother, who in turn must look upon her daughter-in-law as if she is her own daughter. The younger brother is also entitled to be looked upon as the child of the family (emphasis added).

The existing statutory law on Hindu marriage, embodied in the Hindu Marriage Act, 1955 has introduced some changes in the traditional Hindu law of marriage. Thus, it establishes monogamy, provides for restitution of conjugal rights and divorce among others. However, it still remains true that the subject of Hindu marriage is 'more religious than secular' in nature (Jhabvala, 1993). The operation of religious aspects at a deeper and more fundamental level on the issue of marriage is, according to the court in *Saroj Rani v Sudarshan Kumar:*[13]

> In India it must be borne in mind that conjugal rights, that is the right of the husband or the wife to the society of the other spouse is not merely a creature of the statute. Such a right is inherent in the very institution of the marriage itself.

The court further reiterates that as regards the family, it is the 'institution' and not the 'individual' which is of paramount significance. In an even more emphatic decision on the force of religious norms as opposed to those introduced by statute, the court states:

> Introduction of Constitutional Law in the home is most inappropriate. It is like introducing a bull in the China shop. It will be a ruthless destroyer of the marriage institution and all that it stands for. In the privacy of the home and married life, neither Article 21 nor Article 14 have any place. In a sensitive sphere which is at once most intimate and delicate, the introduction of the cold principles of Constitutional Law will have the effect of weakening the marriage bond.[14]

Based upon the judgement, it would follow logically that 'rights' and 'obligations' within marriage must be determined in the context of the institution, which stands for the family that results from the marriage union, rather than the individual. The opposition framed by the court is clearly in these terms, for the named Articles of the Constitution address rights to the individual citizen. In giving this ruling the

---

12 *Ashis v D.C.* AIR 1970 Del 98.

13 AIR 1984 SC 1562.

14 *Harvinder Kaur v Harmander Singh* AIR 1984 Delhi 66.

courts have not merely dealt with the applicability of Articles 14 and 21 of the Indian Constitution, but have gone beyond to reaffirm certain cultural and traditional understandings of the institution of marriage. In doing so, they have brought these traditional understandings within the realm of applied law. Though the Indian personal laws have many elements of religion and culture as explained in the introduction to this chapter, their strength and conviction have coloured the provisions of clearly stated statutory laws.

Moreover, decisions such as those above, exemplify the principle that areas of life hitherto governed and regulated by religion/socio-cultural norms must not be interfered with by statutory law, even if that law is the Constitution. Thus, notwithstanding the post-colonial adoption of new values within the entire legal framework including the Constitution, the above section brings out the recognition of, insistence upon and adherence to the religious and derivative socio-cultural norms that have traditionally defined roles and obligations.

Ownership of Property

Among the various modes of acquisition of property listed in the Manusmriti, such as inheritance, finding or friendly donation, purchase conquest, lending at interest, the performance of work, acceptance of gifts from virtuous men, inheritance is the most important means. Tracing the development of women's right to inherit from the Vedas, there is no single authority for the general position of women regarding inheritance. Various commentators have proposed different, often conflicting opinions on the relevant portions of the Vedas (Mitter, 1984).

Mitter argues that since sacrifices were very important in the Vedic age, and wealth was to be produced for the sake of sacrifices, so long as women were allowed to join in sacrifices, they could acquire property through the various means, including inheritance. However, when the right to participate in sacrifices later came to be denied to women, it may have been that wealth was sought to be diverted from passing to them through inheritance. During the period prior to that of the Manusmriti this would have been the position, as women were no longer held to be competent to recite the Vedas and join in the sacrifices (Mitter, 1984).

Once the relatively equal position of women in the Vedic age had changed into a secondary one at the later time of the *Manusmriti* (believed to be dated around the first century AD), the position regarding the acquisition and ownership of property by females also changed. In this section I will deal expressly with those prescriptions or injunctions addressing the issue of females' right to own property.

The Daughter

As noted earlier, the primary obligation in respect of a daughter is towards her marriage, falling first upon the father, and in his absence, upon the brothers. On her part, she is entitled only to be properly looked after and maintained till she is married. Next, she is entitled to be given away in marriage in order that she fulfil her obligations. Further, upon marriage she becomes part of her husband's family, for she remains in her father's house only so long as she is not married; and as soon as the ceremony is performed she leaves her parents' home for her husband's.

The fact that a daughter is not a constituent member of her father's family is reflected in the Manusmriti's exclusion of the daughter in his dealing of paternal property. On the issue of the partition of paternal property, for instance:

> After the death of the father and of the mother the brothers assembled should divide amongst themselves in equal shares the paternal estate, for they have no power while the parents are alive (Jalali, 1994, 82).

Further, the absence of the daughter's right over paternal property becomes clear with the statement that the unmarried daughters must be given by the brothers a share of the latter's paternal inheritance:

> But to the maiden sisters the brothers shall severally give portions out of their shares, each out of his share one-fourth; those who refuse to give it shall become outcaste (Jalali, 1994, 83).

This statement, made in connection with the allotment of the shares to the unmarried daughters indicates that there is no recognition of the daughter's right in the paternal property, for had the position been the reverse, it would become meaningless. As Das notes, whenever the word 'giving' is used it only signifies that the recipient does not have a legal right or is not the owner of the property concerned (Das, 1993). The words used further indicate that the giving of the one-fourth share to the sisters is more a moral duty of the brothers than a legal one. Further, another statement that the one-fourth share should be given only to the unmarried sisters and nothing to the married ones clarifies that the share given is an allowance for meeting the marriage expenses of the unmarried sisters, it is not a share on account of the daughters having any rights of inheritance in the property of the father.

Therefore, the daughter is not legally entitled to any share in the property of her father; it is only the brothers who contribute severally, parts of their individual shares to her. So in essence the daughter is entitled to share the transferred property of her father, when in the eyes of the law it has become the property of the brothers for all practical purposes. In *Ajit Kumar Maulik v Mukunda Lal Maulik*[15] and *Dharam Singh v Aso*[16] the law was stated as envisaging and allowing for this understanding that a daughter was disentitled from property upon marriage.[17] The disinheritance of daughters upon marriage was seen as a mark of natural dispensation of property, and being equivalent to sons having self supporting incomes in *Khushbir Singh v The State*.[18]

However, even such property as is given by the brothers is not completely at the daughter's disposal. At best, the daughter could have been responsible for its safe custody until her marriage. In ordinary cases the shares given by the brothers could

---

15 AIR 1988 Cal 196.

16 AIR 1990 SC 1888.

17 See also, *Bhagwan Kaur v Chetan Singh* AIR 1988 P & H 198.

18 AIR 1990 Del 59.

have been pooled together and put under the charge of a responsible person who was expected to arrange her marriage with that amount; and she was probably not permitted to take away to her husband's house the residue which would have been left after meeting the marriage expenses. Particularly, if the share had been inclusive of immovable property, it would not have been possible for her to take it away with her (Das, 1993).

Even for the daughter who has no brothers, the Manusmriti does not recognize the right of inheritance or partition in her father's property. Conferring of spiritual benefit on the original owner of the property being the prime consideration, mere blood relationship does not suffice. Although the daughter is as much a blood relation of the parents as the sons, for the purpose of conferring spiritual benefits she is considered inferior to the sons. Crucially, the change of *gotra* which accompanies her marriage makes her unfit to offer *pindas* to her parents. The concept of a share in the property according to the Manusmriti, is in essence a right to a portion of the property as a consequence of the ability and the fitness to confer spiritual benefits on the owner of the property (Das, 1993). Therefore, it justifies the incapacity of even a brotherless daughter to inherit the property of the father.

Thus, in case there are no sons but only daughters, Manu rules that a father shall appoint a daughter and declare, as a procedural formality, that the male child born of her shall perform his funeral rites. The male child in turn, would make spiritual offerings as a son, and become eligible to inherit the property. This provision makes it very clear that the sharer derives the title to the share from his or her capacity to confer spiritual benefits on the original owner of the property (Mukherjee, 1978).

The Wife

According to the Manusmriti, the wife is not entitled to any share in the property of her husband during his lifetime. She has only the right of maintenance against her husband, which could not be denied to her even if she became unchaste, or an outcaste, or persisted in immorality. The wife, the son and the slave are declared to have no property, and the wealth earned by them belong to him to whom they belong (Das, 1993). Specifically regarding the wife,

> … whatever is acquired by the wife belongs to the husband (Mitter, 1984, 276).

Further that:

> Women should never make a hoard from the property which is common to many nor from their own property without their husband's permission (Das, 1993, 96).

The Widow

The Manusmriti does not recognize the widow as the heir to her husband's property, even where he is sonless. It holds that the property of a sonless man will devolve upon his father, then upon his brothers, then the closest male relative and when none of these is forthcoming, first a preceptor, then his disciple and finally the king. The widow is not mentioned in this order of persons. According to Das (1993), the reason for this is that if the property were to be allowed to devolve upon the widow, it would become part of her separate property and further devolved to her daughters, or others, not part of the deceased's family. Thus, with the passing of the property of the deceased to others outside his family, no spiritual benefit could have accrued to the deceased from that property.

As regards maintenance, a widow's right to maintenance out of her husband's property is dependent upon the possession of her husband's property by her husband's heir and conditional upon the chastity of the widow. Thus,

> ... let them allow a maintenance provided they keep unsullied the bed of their lord. But if they behave otherwise, the brother may resume that allowance ... (Mitter, 1984, 421).

There have been instances in traditional Hindu society, before the Hindu Succession Act coming into force wherein the women has been presumed to have absolute ownership over certain kinds of property, like *Stridhana*. However, *Stridhana* was never seen in the context of the women's ownership of immovable property, rather as security against the husbands or in-laws ill-treatment.

Stridhana

The term *Stridhana* is derived from *stri*, woman, and *dhana*, wealth, and according to the Manusmriti, covers:

> What was given before the nuptial fire, what was given on a bridal procession, what was given in token of love, and what was received from her brother, mother or father (Mulla, 1990, 157).

Thus, it is mainly gifts obtained by a woman from her relations, her ornaments and her apparel which constitute her *stridhana*. The only kinds of gifts made from strangers included are presents before the nuptial fire and those made at the bridal procession. Neither gifts from strangers at any other time, nor her acquisitions by her labour and skill constitute her *stridhana*.

Although it would be difficult to show that any Hindu caste or community gave women rights of acquiring, enjoying, and disposing of the property equal to those enjoyed without question by their male relatives, it is important to note that *stridhana* did constitute a concept that distinctly countenanced women's independent ownership. The whole subject, however, was and is a complex one, both in terms of what in fact constituted *stridhana* as well as matters relation to its disposal. Derrett makes the point that on the whole, customs tended to restrict the scope of *stridhana* to the ornaments and clothing actually given to them and inheritance from very near relatives. Further, there was a difference among the various schools on the question of the woman's right to dispose of her *stridhana*. The question whether the property she inherited could be counted as *stridhana* was ultimately determined by the colonial administration, which declared that the inherited property was, with a few exceptions, not *stridhana*, but subject to the limited estate (Derrett, 1970).

Under the present HSA, *Stridhana* is part of the female's property, and loses its separate character. It is thus undifferentiated from any other kind of property which a Hindu female may have ownership over, and the rules regarding its devolution through inheritance are those governing devolution of any property of a female Hindu dying intestate. While it is true that such a uniformity in the application of Hindu law is desirable, there remains a difficulty with the present scheme. In eliminating *stridhana* as a distinct concept, the law simultaneously abolishes the one aspect of independent ownership in respect of females which had hitherto been acknowledged and accepted within Hindu law. Hindu women's right to own property within contemporary society still largely continues to be practised as limited to movables and exclusive of land ownership except in some situations such as gifts. That this limited scope of females' ownership continues to be operative is evident from the increase in the practice of dowry and the justification for the ultimate exclusion of females' ownership of land through inheritance that it provides. Given that the right of females to own property, particularly immovable property, remains to be fully accepted within Hindu society, the inclusion of *stridhana* within the scheme of inheritance has the unfortunate consequence, in fact, of including even such ownership within the scope of that which is exclusionary for the Hindu female. Of course, the argument remains that the objective of the Act is in fact to effect the reverse: that all properties hitherto excluded from women's ownership are to be given the same scope for legitimacy as obtained for *stridhana*. However, the reality of women's continued, in fact increased, exclusion, in addition to the fact that exclusion was the predominant principle to which *stridhana* was the exception, therefore overweighing the reformative objective of establishing ownership for females, perhaps leaves the conclusion arguable.

Models, Roles and Identity

Thus far, I have dealt with specific aspects of women's roles and obligations within the Hindu Shastras which have formed the basis of law in the context of the development of Hindu law, both statutory and through judicial decisions. How do these understandings and analyses illuminate the reality that may constitute women's lives? To what extent can they be said to reflect the values and expectation, roles and obligations, of Hindu women in Indian society today, and therefore, to what extent does law reflect and perpetuate a certain identity of Hindu women? What can be said to be the predominant aspects of such identity? In this section, I shall attempt to address these issues by an analysis of some of the aspects of Hindu women's identity that is implicit in the legal framework.

The legal provisions under the HSA and the changes sought to be introduced therein, are based upon a more individualistic notion of property (Sharma, 1990), both in terms of ownership of land by an individual rather than the corporate group of the joint Hindu family, and in the underlying assumption that persons to whom rights are addressed can act as individuals separate from the family. In relation to women's position specifically under the Act, the women are addressed as the daughter in respect of her interest vis-à-vis the father, a sister in relation to her right in conjunction with the sons and the widow. Further, the relations posited within the scheme are based upon the following assumptions in respect of women's position and role as the daughter, sister and widow.

First, that as a daughter she continues to be a member, socially, culturally and factually, of her parents' family. Second, that as such a member of her parents' family she has an interest, both perceived and legitimate in her parents' property. Third, that such interest is perceived in terms of her interest individually, exclusive of the social relations that may otherwise define her position, and finally, that as a sister, she has an interest in a claim that puts her in competition with her brother.

These assumptions are in fact not borne out in the social reality of women's lives, and that the framework of law promoting the principles as it does, in fact contributes to the these effects. In discussing aspects of women's lives, I take recourse to analyses and discussions from fields other than law, for while judicial materials have much to add to the sociologists understanding of Indian family and kinship, a comparative sociological approach can throw important light on the culture of the modern Hindu family law in both its theory and practice (Uberoi, 1995).

A Hindu woman's identity evolves out of the particulars of her life cycle and childhood, out of the everyday relationships as daughter in her parents' family and as wife and daughter-in-law in her husband's family. It is equally affected by the universals of traditional ideals of womanhood absorbed by her from childhood onwards (Kakar, 1996). Kakar further makes the observation that although in most societies a woman, more than a man, defines herself in relation and connection to other people, this is singularly true of Indian women: her identity is wholly defined by her relationships to others. First she is a daughter to her parents. Secondly she is a wife to her husband (and daughter in-law to his parents). Third, she is a mother to her sons (and daughters) (Kakar, 1996).

A daughter's birth within the household is not welcomed traditionally, as the various references in the religious texts show, highlighted in the previous section. Contemporary anthropological studies from different parts of India (Mandelbaum, 1970; Madan, 1994) and the available clinical evidence assure us that the traditional preference for sons is very much intact. At the birth of a son drums are beaten in some parts of the country, conch shells are blown in others and the midwife paid lavishly, while no such spontaneous rejoicing accompanies the birth of a daughter. Traditional households still perform ancient rites on the pregnant woman to elicit the birth of a male child. There is also sufficient evidence of the extremes that this preference can take, in the practices of female infanticide and the use of amniocentesis against the birth of a female child (Krisnaswamy, 1996; Patel, 1996). These practices are very much an expression of the scriptural values, as Krisnaswamy notes, in response to the superiority of sons for religious rites, particularly the obligation and ability of only a son to perform ritual oblations for the soul of the deceased parents.

This explicit undesirability of a female child, at least in preference of boys, is made clear to almost every girl in a Hindu household. The effect is that the cultural devaluation of girls may in turn be internalized by the female through her experience. Kakar (1996) argues, from a psycho-social perspective, of the possibility that girls and women may transform the cultural devaluation into feelings of worthlessness and inferiority. Similarly, Nandy, taking the example of lower survival rate for girls than boys, suggests that it is a function of maternal neglect, a weird expression of woman's hostility toward womanhood and also, symbolically, toward her own self (Nandy, 1996).

The feelings of inferiority generated in girls in comparison with boys within a family are compounded by the extension of ideology of devaluation: where the daughter becomes a burden to her parents. Underlying this is the idea that a girl does not 'belong' to her parents' family; that she is a 'guest' only for a temporary period, and that her 'real' home is with her husband's family. Madan, in his study of the rural pandits in Kashmir, notes that an unmarried female (agnate) is always referred to as 'amanat', that is as someone held in trust on behalf of her lawful owners. A young girl's upbringing is completely overshadowed by the fact that she is to be married and sent away to live with her husband and parents-in-law (Madan, 1994). Before marriage, her parent's home is her home too, and in the span of a few hours, after the marriage, she becomes a stranger to it and in fact the house of strangers, her in-laws' home, is supposed to become her home. In time, it does, as she begins to participate in the domestic life. At the same time, the position of the wife as a 'newcomer' or stranger is never totally overcome, although it may be that she also acquires other positions as mother, mistress of the house, mother-in-law, and so on (Mandelbaum, 1970; Madan, 1994).[19]

Marriage, therefore bestows upon a woman the enduring status in her life. It requires of her to relinquish her emotional attachment and expectations that come naturally in respect of her parents' family and inculcate a similar sentiment towards her husband's family (Mandelbaum, 1970). The task is acknowledged to be difficult, and is brought out by the duty of a mother to teach the necessary virtues to her daughter, who must learn to be a good wife in order to be good woman. Srinivas writes of the women in Mysore:

> … It is the mother's duty to train her daughter to be an absolute docile daughter-in-law. The summnum bonum of a girl's life is to please her parents-in-law and her husband. If she does not "get on" with her mother-in-law she will be a disgrace to her family, and cast a blot on the fair name of her mother. The Kannada mother dins it into her daughter's ears certain ideals which make for harmony (at the expense of sacrificing her will) in later life… (Srinivas 1942 in Kakar, 1996, 51).

A girl's membership in her parent's family is undesired at worst, and temporary at best. The dominant role for the Hindu woman is that of the wife and her position as a wife and daughter-in-law is subservient and that of a stranger at least to begin with, but it assumes a permanence, and in time, the woman may well feel less an outsider.

---

19 The case of *Chandania v Gyan Chand* AIR 1989 All. 75 highlights the reality and endurance of this alienation of a Hindu wife in her husband's home. In this case, a man left only maintenance rights to his wife and all his property to his nephew under a will. Here, the court acknowledged that the property may be passed to a member of his 'own' family by a man through a will, to prevent its being passed on to his widow and members of 'her' family.

A significant, related aspect is that throughout her development, from childhood to marriage and after, the essence of a woman's identity is to be traced in its relation to others. As said earlier, she is a daughter, wife, sister, mother and so on, particularly in relation to the male. The ideals of womanhood in each of these roles, and the achievement of these ideals, primarily through acquiescence and submissiveness, docility at the risk of sacrificing her own will and interest are both aspects that reinforce and support one another. As Kakar points out,

> ... In addition to the "virtues" of self-effacement and self-sacrifice, the feminine role in India also crystallises a woman's connection to others, her embeddedness in a multitude of familial relationships (Kakar, 1996, 51).

Chitnis notes (1996) that the ideology of personal freedom is new to both men and women in India, who have hitherto functioned under rigid hierarchies and learned to curb their freedom. Where they have conditioned themselves to suppress their needs, silence their senses and sublimate their selves in a philosophy of self-denial and self-effacement and service,

> ... The challenge to feminism in India is to help Indian woman realise their self-hood, personal freedom and autonomy in full measure (Chitnis, 1996, 94).

Finally, the precarious position of the wife, in the husband's family, where she has to 'earn' her position and respect, bound by manifold duties and obligations, and strive to achieve the ideals inculcated in her for her 'happiness' – leaves her dependent on her brothers in case of ill-treatment by her in-laws, or desertion by her husband. The special relation between brothers and sisters, marked by the brothers' duty to protect his sister and the sister's special dependence on him to do so is marked by millions of Hindu males and females every year in the festival of 'Rakhee'. The festival is the celebration of the brother-sister relationship, where the ritual consists of a sister tying a piece of thread on her brother's wrist as a symbol of lifelong affection, in return for which the brother is bound by a duty to always come to her protection.

Conclusion

To conclude, changes in the legal provisions affirming women's equal right to inheritance in the parents' property would require the existence of the following aspects of the cultural and social reality of Hindu women in India.

Firstly, the identification of her personhood independent of her relations to others in the family, secondly the continuing identity of a woman as a member of her parents' family even after marriage, and in which she can therefore have a legitimate expectation, and finally, the willingness of women, as sisters, to jeopardize their relations with brothers and the security they may expect thereby, by competing with brothers for the same interest in land.

In fact, this is not the reality. The assumptions upon which the law is based continue to be unrealized, and in this, the law itself plays a significant part. The erasure of the daughter's claim as a *necessary component* of Hindu identity in the case of *K. Devabalan v M. Vijaykumari*[20] is the clearest disjunction between Hindu women's identity, even as constructed by law, as their entitlement to hold property. The decisions noted earlier throw into question whether one can even assert the existence of a 'legal' entitlement even in the face of contradictory exposition of the legal provision by the courts. Where

> Ideology is, in part, a representational process whereby beliefs, images, attributions and explanations are constructed historically in conjunction with, and in relation to, material and cultural conditions and power relations, but are presented as natural, inevitable and necessary in the current conjuncture (Kline, 1994, 451).

Hindu cultural ideology makes women's subservient, dependent and familial role normative to the extent that there is very limited scope for the emergence of women's interests as individuals and independent of relations to others. Although the reformative aspects in legal provisions are aimed at changing this to some extent, the legal provisions in fact operate to negative the impact, by incorporating and promoting those very aspects of women's position and social role that militate against it. The application of law by the courts reinforces this, in that it is often informed by the dominant conceptions of the family, or 'familial ideology', through which the ideas about what the family is, and what roles the people play within the family are universalized and naturalized (Kapur and Cossman, 1998, 68).

> The family is presented both in law and popular culture as the basic unit in society, a sacred, timeless and so natural an institution that its definition is self evident (Gavigan, 1988, 293).

Moreover, this dominant conception of the family also includes a set of assumptions about the roles and responsibilities of the family members, roles and responsibilities which are allocated strictly on the basis of gender. Women are allocated the role of wives and mothers – they are responsible for child care and domestic labour. The role of law in reinforcing these roles even as it institutes them as independent property holders is reflected in *Parnam Balaji v Bathina Venkataramayya*.[21] In this case, the court investigated the 'adult' position of a Hindu woman within the family under Hindu law, holding that she could not in fact occupy any adult role in a Hindu family, having no rights to adult status. Hindu cultural ideology has even laid down modes of behaviour, morals, duties and obligations specific to gender and marital status.

Finally, in evaluating women's self-interest in land ownership, it would be difficult to conclude that the law, both in its statutory expression, as well as religious and cultural norms, fosters such an interest. While ostensibly the law is premised upon the existence of such interest, it in fact reinforces the ideology that excludes it. To the extent the changes introduced in the law to promote females' proprietary rights may be alien to a significant number of Hindu women.

---

20 AIR 1991 Ker 175.
21 AIR 1988 AP 250.

This leads to the perception of law as an imposition of alien values, and therefore makes the law ineffective in changing attitudes and values where the rightness of the law is questioned (Parasher, 1992, 31).

Further, in so far as religious and traditional values and principles continue to inform the life views and worlds of Hindu women as brought out in the last and current chapter,

> … Their replacement by any other values is bound to be resisted, particularly because, for the majority of women, issues of equal rights and feminism do not have any reality (Parasher, 1992, 35).

The legal framework in fact strengthens the lack of females' individual self-interest to claim a share in parental property. To the extent that self-interest does exist to claim a share in the property of the marital family, such interest is effectively ignored within the legal framework. The resulting position is one where the law, although it seeks to enhance Hindu women's independent ownership of property, including land, by its very framework ultimately serves to perpetuate women's inability to own land. Its emphasis upon Hindu religious norms leads to its construction of women's claim to land as addressed to 'Hindu' women and family property through succession. As such, it fails to establish a basis for their self-interest to a claim in land, so constructed.

Chapter 6

Women, Work and Land Rights

Introduction

The previous chapters have explored the construction of women's claim to land by law within religious ideology. The basis upon which such claim must be constructed, it has been argued, must be not only in ideological terms, but also the material bases. This means that the lived experiences of women, their material reality as labourers, workers and contributors must be accounted for. It requires recognition of the ways and means in which women are engaged in these processes of work and production and analyses of the structures which sustain, strengthen or jeopardize these. The bargaining approach enables us to expand the construction within law, shown to be ideologically biased, and include perceptions of women's work and contribution as a factor affecting claims to resources. This section discusses women's work as it affects their claim to land and addresses the second aspect of the 'dichotomy' in constructing women's claim to land — as addressed to peasant women, within the household, affected by their work and contribution to agricultural production.

The relation between women's access to land and perceptions of women's contributions to income from land can be argued to be directly linked. In the specific context of the class of small and medium farming households within the agricultural sector, the extent to which law recognizes women's contribution in production, and thereby promotes their ability to negotiate access to land will be discussed. As we have seen in the previous chapter, Hindu women's right to individual shares through inheritance is statutorily guaranteed, although such right does not in fact resonate with the cultural ideology, and women's lived realities, identities and interests. Following the argument made there, that Hindu women's right to ownership does not correspond to the socio-cultural reality upon which the law also seeks to and does operate, this chapter argue that in addition, law also does not reflect the socio-economic reality of women's lives that they are significant actors in agricultural production.

This section analyses the extent to which the legal framework does or does not take account of women's contributions to production from land. To draw out the possible interaction between work contribution and bargaining power over resources, literature drawn from the fields of economics and development policy has been useful. Whereas the focus of writers within these fields has often not included law, they provide useful frameworks and analysis relevant for analysis of law. In his analysis of gender and co-operative conflicts, Sen (1987, 1985) has argued that the informational base of the bargaining problem has to be widened to include perceptions of legitimacy and desert. Whereas the exclusive focus on individual interests and the assumption of clear and unambiguous perceptions of these interests are limited, missing crucial aspects of the nature of gender divisions within and outside the family, the bargaining approach must take account of

> ... The sense of appropriateness (that) goes hand in hand with ambiguities of perceptions of interests, and with certain perceived notions of legitimacy regarding what is "deserved" and what is not (Sen, 1987, 17).

Sen further explains that the impact of 'perceived contribution response' may have been associated with acquiring food from outside. The fact that the sexual division of labour allocates tasks based upon social constructions of gender, and that such construction typically allows males to do the work of 'acquiring' food, while females are involved in other activities, may not in fact weaken the *perception of special importance of bringing the food home* (emphasis added; Sen, 1987). This seems to have been supported by Boserup's observation that women fare relatively better in societies where they play a major role in bringing food from outside (Boserup, 1970). Again, studies of women's role in the paid labour force, particularly in agriculture, have been based on the understanding that a woman's role in providing for the family from external means, and not from work within her own household has increased visibility and therefore greater impact on her status as provider (Bordahn, 1985). The underlying assumption is that since women have an income, they have control over certain economic resources which they may then manipulate in negotiating their socio-economic status within the household. This assumption has been summed up:

> Whether one views the increase in female agriculture labourers as an indicator of growing rural poverty or as a positive sign that more agricultural work is available for women, its effect in terms of our third criterion (i.e. decision making) should be examined separately. Evidence suggests that the increased paid employment outside the home may actually improve the women's bargaining position within the family (Bennett 1989 in Bagchi and Raju, 1993, 180).

In the conditions of subsistence and overwhelming dependence on land as the means of livelihood that is pertinent to small and medium farming households, the evidence from a vast number of studies shows that families live in near-poverty, and land is the resource that provides the maximum security against absolute poverty. In this context, ownership of the scarce resource that is land is fraught with contestations and the social legitimacy of a claim is related to cultural norms as well as economic realities. It has to be remembered that the 'family' addressed within the HSA is also, for most cases, the unit of subsistence production, the 'household'. The existing legal framework for the inter-generational transfer of property collapses the functions and normative structural differences adhering to these within a single unit, the family. In other words, the law does not envisage the 'family' as the site for both *production* as well as *reproduction*. Transmission of property through generation is a function of social reproduction which succession and inheritance law can be seen to promote. However, the extent to which this process of social reproduction is made possible, viable and therefore valuable by processes of *production* is obscured by the current legal framework. While the family and the household have thus far not been distinguished precisely for this reason, this section is based on the recognition that there must be a clear analytical distinction in considering the family and the household as the locus of subsistence production. As Sangari notes on the inadequacy of discussion on the issue of domestic labour, 'studies on India foreground its "economic" nature but have rarely discussed its "productive" dimension in strict theoretical terms' (Sangari, 1999, 280). Whereas gender ideology biased against the female can operate pervasively across both, the operation of gender ideology in subsistence production is predicated, in addition to culturally defined gender relations, upon relations of production.

Although the relations of production at the subsistence level within a capitalist framework have implications for the value assigned to such production (Mies, 1980; Beneria and Sen, 1981; Elson and Pearson, 1981; Sharma, 1986; Omvedt, 1994; Benholdt-Thomson and Mies, 1999), and in the case of India, particularly for home-based workers for export (Mies, 1981), and landless labourers in agriculture, what is relevant for our purposes is the normative separation of the family as a separate private sphere, from productive processes in the opposite public sphere. Further, the sexual division of labour within most societies predicates that women are located within this 'domestic' sphere, while men go out of it to do 'productive work' (Harris: 50). In the particular case of women in household or home based production, the issue becomes more difficult due to location of the productive sphere as well as the family within the same physical space, leading to a submersion of women's productive role within their role as the nurturer. This exacerbates the non-visibility of women's role in income creation or contribution to the family's survival and sustenance.

Where the issue of land ownership is sought to be determined by law on the basis of gender, the legitimacy of such a law must be not only based on cultural norms and values, but also relations of production. The social legitimacy of a claim must be based on both these aspects in order to improve a person's bargaining position. On this issue the framework provided by Sen, taking account of women's role in production, and the need to enhance perceptions of their contribution to production/ income provides a strategy that may be developed through appropriate policy. Agarwal argues that although enhancing perceptions of women's contributions may be achieved the outcome may cease to be positive if the legitimacy of a claim is based upon need rather than contributions, the problem being amplified where culturally defined notions of needs may also be gender-biased.

Although this is a valid point, particularly in societies such as India where culturally defined gender identities may be deep rooted among most people, it does not, in my view, lessen the significance of the role that perceptions of contributions do play in ascribing legitimacy (Sangari, 1999). Further, Agarwal's argument is perhaps also relevant to a subsequent stage in policy analysis after perceptions of women's role in production have in fact been enhanced, since, as the following sections develop, we do not yet have a policy focus on women's contribution with the aim of enhancing perceptions of the same.

The issue of land ownership and control has two very different sets of implications in the context of women in agriculture. First, the relationship of those who do not own any land, but work on it as wage labourers for others is characterized by the absence of ownership over any land. Here the issue is one of redistribution or allocation of land through land reform policies establishing ownership and control for sections of the agricultural producers that hitherto had no land. Secondly, once land comes to be owned by an individual, ownership may then be transmitted to heirs including females, through succession. Women's work in agriculture may be classed according to the two contexts: women working as hired labourers primarily where they themselves do not have access to land for their own cultivation, or at least, not sufficient land, and women working as cultivators on their own land, or that owned by their husbands/fathers.

This discussion focuses on the evaluation of women's work as cultivators, on land owned by themselves or their husband/fathers. Here the question of women having independent ownership and control to their lawful share becomes an issue of intra-household bargaining and negotiation, being affected by gender relations within the household and notions of legitimacy, including perceived contribution. It is the issue of women's effective ownership and control over the land where they have a legal right to own the land; for instance where the land is owned by a member of the family, of which the woman is a member and on which land she works. It is for this category of women that problems regarding evaluation of their work, and therefore their role in the agricultural production are heightened. To begin with, the classification of their work becomes a problem, as to whether it is domestic work, household work, leisure work or economically productive in agriculture? Secondly the evaluation of their work is ambiguous, in so far as their work is seen to be a necessity or otherwise in determining the level of agricultural productivity and income for the household. Thirdly, there is no specific remuneration that may provide an index of the cost/benefit to the family.

Cultural Ideology and Perceptions of Women's Contribution

Although research on working women or women with access to an income, links employment to a higher status in terms of female welfare and autonomy, there are studies pointing towards the contrary, that gender hierarchy is so rigid within the household that mere wage labour of women does not guarantee a shift of balance in power relations between genders (Ahmed-Ghosh, 1993). Sharma's study of Punjab and Himachal Pradesh makes the similar point that the women's wage labour in itself is controlled by household members and not by the women themselves. She explains:

> In theory we might certainly expect to find that women who work for wages (and even women who work as family labourers) have a greater say in the household matters than women who perform their domestic work only, and this is an assumption that has often been made both by anthropologists and others. But the female labourer usually earns wages which are too small and sporadic to lend her any special leverage in household politics, and the work of the female family labourers does not give women any particular control over the products of their labour (Sharma, 1980, 196).

The research on women's work has exposed the dialectical link between women's work and the cultural context within which it exists (Bardhan, 1985; Mazumdar and Sharma, 1990; Gleason, 1991; Mencher, 1993; Agarwal, 1994). Gender relations are defined by cultural ideology to construct women's subordinate position, to the extent that their resources in terms of labour, time and productivity are controlled by males (Bardhan, 1985; Sharma, 1985; Jha et al., 1998).

Cultural ideology determines not only the perception of others regarding the women's work and contribution, but also that of the women themselves. Although Sen's framework focuses on the former, Agarwal points out that the perceptions of women themselves are also relevant to determine the basis of legitimacy of a claim. Nonetheless, it would appear that the effect of others' perceptions based upon the prevailing cultural ideology on the perceived legitimacy of a claim by women themselves is such that, while women *do* have a conviction and perception of themselves as equal workers and contributors, this does not enhance the legitimacy of their individual claim. Women belonging to households at subsistence level do not distinguish between 'productive' labour and household work and claim that 'all the work that they do is for the family' (see Chapter 4; Ghosh, 1993, 192; Sangari, 1999).[1] However they do consider themselves to be workers equal to men in providing for the family. The reasons for this have been suggested by Bhattacharya who asserts that the asset base of the households at subsistence level is so small that most of the production is for household consumption. Bhattacharya maintains that:

> because total production work input of the household members will be much less in such [subsistence] households as compared to that in the households having larger asset bases, the contribution of women members of the households as participants in generating the non-marketed products can only be small in absolute size, however crucial it might be to the survival of the household. The separate identity of this marginal work, which in major cases is performed only intermittently together with women's other work of housekeeping, is more often likely to be lost in reckoning. In effect the work becomes "invisible" (Bhattacharya, 1985, 200).

In the context of women's work in rice cultivation, Mencher (1993) explores the concept of 'hard work' in the context of south Asian agriculture. Focusing on data from two of the southern states (Kerala and Tamil Nadu) and one state in the east (West Bengal), the question she raises is: how has it come about that women's work is regarded as easier than men's work, both by the workers themselves and by many social scientists who study them? Who is doing the defining and what are the criteria being used? Taking the lead from Agarwal (1988b), she looks at the dialectical relationship between the material context of women's relationship to agriculture and the land on one hand, and gender ideology (here related to the valuation placed on what work they do in agriculture) on the other.

She points out that for both males and females, actual participation in manual field work has always been culturally considered to be degrading, and withdrawal from fieldwork has always been associated with higher socio-economic class. Further, tasks in field work have always been segregated by gender in South Asia. For example, although in addition to the many tasks they perform in rice cultivation

---

1   As I have discussed in Chapter 4, the responses of women in my field research were in identical terms, where they do not conceptualize their work in individual terms, but as being 'for the family'.

women may also plant vegetables and work the soil manually, they have rarely been considered worthy to plough the fields. The study also highlights the existing belief among women that only men should be allowed to plough since ploughing has to be done with sanctity or by those who are sacred. By implication, women, who by nature menstruate should not, as those who menstruate pollute the earth (Mencher, 1993). In my study, notwithstanding women's acknowledged role as workers of equivalent significance, the respondents justified men's primary position on the ground that only they could do ploughing, which was 'most difficult work', 'too difficult for women', which 'women could never be able to do'.[2]

The link between value placed upon types of work, which at first sight appear to be on non-gendered, objective criteria, such as difficulty or skill, and gender is significant. Upon examination, it becomes clear that the characterization of different types of work and values associated with them are in fact highly gendered. Giving the example of pulling seedlings in Tamil Nadu and Kerala, Mencher points out that pulling the seedling for transplantation is considered to be 'hard work' where men do it in Tamil Nadu but 'easy work' in Kerala, where it is women who do it. She also notes that in many areas where only women are expected to transplant, most men would refuse to carry out this work even if there is no other work for them on various grounds. Among these, it might be asserted, for example, that only the women knew how to do it or that it was 'women's work' or easy work – even though in another region the task may be classed as 'men's work' or as gender neutral.

The value placed on women's work in agriculture as well as other sectors, bears a relation to the visibility of such work that is mutually reinforcing. In its negative operation, as in the case of agricultural workers and cultivators in India, work that is not valued within the social framework remains invisible as it is not taken into account, and its invisibility perpetuates underestimation and undervaluation (Beneria, 1988). Taken together, this has a direct effect on perceptions of women's contribution and the ultimate effect is one where the contribution made by women by virtue of their unrecognized and undervalued activities is also perceived to be very low or non-existent.

Evaluating Women's Work in Agriculture

Agriculture accounted for over 35 per cent India's Gross National Product (GNP) in 1980–1981 and around 23 per cent in 2001–2002 and employs three-quarters of all economically active women (Agarwal, 2003; World Bank, 2006). Seventy-five per cent of all female workers and 85 per cent of all rural female workers are in agriculture (Agarwal, 2003). The past two decades have seen a steady increase in women's share of agricultural employment, leading to what some have called the 'feminization' of agriculture (UNRISD, 2005). Despite this increased dependence on women's economic productivity, they are less endowed with resources in terms of health, education and most importantly the primary productive resources such

---

2   I have discussed women's responses in my own research, particularly their attitudes and understanding of 'work', the value placed on such work and other issues previously, in Chapter 4.

as land. As Jackson (2003) notes, the feminization of agriculture is not the same as feminization of farm management. The growing concentration of women in agricultural wage labour is more about women's involvement in laborious, worst paid and low status work than greater control and access to other resources. Therefore, at one end of the policy spectrum we see the pervasive lack of human resource endowment and at the other we see the women not having ownership of land due to the predominantly traditional, religious and social requirement for patrilineal transmission of property. Hence the situation is of subsistence requiring high levels of work participation, but with the absence of control over the primary means of subsistence namely land.

This absence of women as independent providers/workers, has been the result of a lack of identification and acknowledgement of the corresponding work participation, at the same time it has determined the way in which they have characterized their work. This is further deepened by reinforced ideas of women as 'dependants' or supplementary to family subsistence requirements. Moreover, this cycle has led to women's own underestimation, not to mention the gross underestimation and invisibility of the women's work in official and other studies. Studies during the last decades have brought to light the nature and extent of women's work participation in subsistence and agricultural labour (Bardhan, 1985; Sardamoni, 1988, Mies 1986; Bagchi, 1993). It is important to affirm that this remains true today, and that in fact women's involvement in the agricultural labour is increasing (Statistical Profile of Women Labour, 1993; Agarwal, 2003). To quote Mencher,

> … women perform a very large part of the heavy manual work in rice cultivation in India. This is important to note because as compared to the African and South-East Asian women in agriculture, the involvement of Indian women in the field has often been ignored (Mencher, 1993, 99).

That there still exists this gap in recognizing women's work for what it is may be brought out by how their work has been classified or understood, in the policies and plans of the state. Mies (1986) brings out the point that development programme for women focus on women not as peasants or wage workers, but as property-less petty commodity workers. Whether they hold land, or have the potential to do so by law and individual circumstances, essentially makes no difference to how women work, and therefore characterized, since the fact remains that by and large they do not control the land. In my own study in Orissa, I was given a puzzled look by the District Commissioner when I asked if there were any programmes for women *as cultivators* or *peasants*. The response was to list the various programmes 'for the development of women', such as milch cattle development, milk co-operatives, basket making and the like, and again, the concept of women working in agriculture was clearly *not* as cultivators but petty commodity producers or in allied activities. This section draws upon the issues around women's work in agriculture: what constitutes 'work' as performed by women; the activities that have been documented as work done by women; the process of statistical enumeration whereby women's work comes to be defined.

Issues in Conceptualizing and Enumerating Women's Work

The population that has the ability and willingness to work constitutes the labour force. However, who is actually included in the work force would very much depend upon how 'work' is defined in such accounting. This section addresses the issues raised by the means through which women's work in agricultural production is presently enumerated and evaluated in official studies. This includes the manner in which women's work is first of all conceptualized as predominantly 'domestic', and therefore unproductive, and secondly, the translation of this limited understanding into under-enumeration and under representation of women's work in official statistics and data collection through exclusion of large areas of women's work.

Existing studies show that the work and contribution of women, particularly in agricultural production, is not accurately reflected in official data, where the more 'economic' and traditionally technical parameters of measurement have been used. The result is a logical exclusion of all activities outside the market mainstream as 'peripheral' and 'non-economic' (Beneria, 1988). Since most of the pre-harvest and post-harvest operations in which women participate are carried out at home, a large number of self employed women are excluded from the count. In addition allied agricultural activities such as dairying, poultry farming, along with the survival tasks of firewood/fodder collection and procurement of water are not considered work if they are for self-consumption.

In India, the National Sample Survey Organisation (NSSO) has been more sensitive in its attempt to capture women's contribution to work by adopting multiple approaches to define economic activities. For example, its 32nd, 38th, and 43rd rounds (conducted in 1977−78, 1983, 1987−88) introduced innovative measures such as inclusion and division of domestic workers into two categories. First, those engaged in 'domestic duties' only (activity code No. 92) and the second, those who 'attend domestic duties and [were] also engaged in free collection of goods (vegetables, roots, firewood, cattle feed, and so on), sewing, tailoring, weaving, and so on for household use' (activity code No. 93) (Sen and Sen, 1985; Raju, 1993). For this an exclusive set of probing questions for those who where categorized as 'usually engaged in household duties' was adopted to elicit information on their participation in certain specific activities for household consumption.[3] By including the latter category, female labour participation rates are brought considerably closer to that for the men (Sen and Sen, 1985).

Apart from cooking cleaning, child care, and looking after the aged and the sick which may fall within the 'pure' domestic sphere, several categories of work which are predominantly performed by women in rural and urban India clearly have components that are not 'pure' domestic work. These include: (a) self-employment in

---

3   These activities were: maintenance of kitchen garden, orchards, and so on, work in household poultry and dairy, free collection of fish, small game, and so on, free collection of firewood, husky paddy, preparation of jaggery, grinding of food grains, preparation of cow-dung cakes to be used as fuel, sewing and tailoring, tutoring of children, bringing water from outside the household premise and outside the village (Sen and Sen, 1985; Raju, 1993).

cultivation for own consumption, (b) subsistence dairy and livestock rearing, fishing, hunting, and cultivation of fruit and vegetable gardens, (c) fetching fuel, fodder and water, repair of dwellings, making of cow dung cakes, and food preservation. In addition, women's work in 'informal' health care is particularly invisible in official statistics (Krishnaraj, 1989; UNRISD, 2005).

The definition of 'work' determines who is counted as a 'worker' (Gleason, 1991). According to the Government of India's Statistical Profile on Women Labour (1993), which has been compiled from the data collected in the 1991 Census, the term 'Worker', defines a person whose main activity was participation in any economically productive activity. Such participation could be physical or mental in nature. Work involved not only actual work but also effective supervision and direction of work. It also includes unpaid work on the farm or family enterprise. However the workers were further categorized as 'main' and 'marginal', depending on whether they had worked for a total of six months or more in a year. This can lead to certain anomalies in the rural context since agricultural work is very often seasonal and may not require six months or more for crop production.

In the case of census data the example of definitional effects can be seen in the sharp decline of women's labour force participation in 1971 as compared to 1961. The reference period by which status as a worker was identified varied in the two counts. In 1971, respondents were asked to identify their 'main activity' which, given the nature of women's work would often elicit the response of 'housewife' (Raju, 1993), resulting in the said decline in female participation rates in 1971 (Mathur, 1994). In 1981, and 1991 the 'usual status' approach was adopted, were the question asked, was have you 'worked any time at all last year?' In case of affirmative answer, the respondents were asked what their main activities were. Those who worked for at least 183 days (six months) in the preceding one year were treated as main workers and those who did not work for this period were treated as marginal workers. Nevertheless, the definition of 'Work' in the 1991 Census does not take into consideration the household work done by the women, providing an example of how definitions can substantially alter the identification and recognition of the work done by women (Raju, 1993; Mathur, 1994). The World Bank (1991) notes that there is a 'statistical purdah' imposed by the existing methods of measuring labour force participation which renders much of the women's work invisible. The lack of precision in defining and measuring what is meant by 'subsistence or household production' and 'domestic' work has led to very different answers to the question of where Indian women are working. In the specific context of agricultural work, this was echoed by the Report of the Committee on the Status of Women in India (1975, 162):

> While Census data classifies agricultural workers into only two categories, namely, cultivators and labourers, this classification does not, in fact, reflect the realities of the agricultural community.

The published data on female labour is dogged with the problems of under-enumeration and conceptual flaws as well as inconsistent and inadequate measurement frameworks. This invisibility in the data is actually a reflection on misplaced societal perception of female labour as of secondary consequence and the male as the primary bread-winner, despite conflicting evidence (Agarwal, 1985; Gleason, 1991; Bagchi and Raju, 1993). In her study of the lace-makers of Narsapur Mies highlights the fact that definitions of women's work tend to obscure the amount, the intensity and the productivity of female work (Mies, 1982). There are aspects of women's work which can come under conventional categorization but there is substantially a lot more which is excluded and fails to be accounted for. Further and most importantly, this work done by women, although seemingly irrelevant to conventional frameworks and accounting methods, has a direct correlation to the agricultural productivity and the total income of the household and therefore impact upon the well-being of the family.

The various studies undertaken in the past three decades identifying and highlighting the whole range of tasks done by the women and the need to include that as 'productive work', has resulted in the growing sensitivity towards female contribution in non-wage activities. For example, the Indian census in 1991, has attached an explicit rider in the identification of workers to include 'unpaid work on the farm or in family enterprise'. Nevertheless, it is clear that the problems of enumeration and statistical accounts to encompass the range of activities carried out by women in agriculture as 'work' are a reflection of the difficulties in conceptualizing what constitutes 'work' as done by women. Indeed, as Ginwala et al. (1990) point out, the reasons why women's work 'vanishes' in economic and policy analysis are the ignorance and undervaluation that are prevalent as regards women's work. Statistical exclusion leads to the undervaluation through under-enumeration, while this process is reinforced by ignorance of the daily tasks and activities that women in fact carry out. As Bardhan notes:

> The underestimation of peasant women's economically productive work is more than a statistical problem that concerns planners and policy makers. It reflects and legitimises the devaluation of female labour in the household economy of peasants, helping the process of male-controlled accumulation (Bardhan, 1985, 2214).

The argument Bardhan makes above is critical to the argument this books makes. Work, or what is recognized to be work, is argued to be a crucial basis for the legitimacy of ownership and other forms of control. To the extent that ownership of assets is predominantly male, it is supported by the legitimacy of (male) 'work' and the delegitimization of (women's) work. In such a context, any effort to redress the male bias in ownership and redesign the basis of ownership of assets must necessarily address the exclusion of women's work and contribution. In the context of peasant households therefore, legislative changes, discussed in previous chapters, to ensure greater gender equality in ownership can succeed only if supported by a greater recognition of women's work. The legitimacy and therefore acceptance of any changes to accord greater rights to women will require support from greater recognition and valuation of women's work. Towards this, the next section highlights the range of women's tasks, which need to be included in any discussion of women's work.

What Is Women's Work?

Traditionally, the definition of work is oriented towards capturing some form of remuneration or profit in return for labour and includes those who are engaged in a) wage and salaried employment, b) self-employment outside the household for profit, and c) self-employment in cultivation and household industries for profit (Raju, 1983; Benaria, 1988; Gleason, 1991). Unpaid activity, where a significant proportion of goods and services are produced for self consumption, results in the exclusion of the wide range of activities not geared towards exchange and market from the definition of 'work'. As these are for self consumption, they assume significance particularly at the subsistence level (Bardhan, 1985; Mukhopadhyay, 1985; Baneria, 1988; Gleason, 1991; Bgachi and Raju, 1993). To counteract this, the Indian census counts cultivation of crops as 'work' even if it is for self consumption. However, the gulf between male and female participation rates continues because even in agriculture much of the related activity resulting in produce for self-consumption, primarily undertaken by the women, are invisible and cannot be captured by the existing concept of work.

Suggestions to increase the consideration of 'work' to include women's participation include the counting of all household work such as cooking, cleaning, tailoring, child and elderly care as economic activities. This would be on the basis that all these have a price in that they can be substituted for goods and services which would otherwise be paid for (Gleason, 1991; Bagchi, 1993). However Bagchi also remarks that while it would make the role of women in the economy visible,

> ... it (would) also cloud the real issues and a certain complacency may ensue because female labour would then no longer be invisible (Bagchi, 1993, 5).

Measuring Women's Work in Agriculture

Sen has argued that the perception of contribution has to be distinguished from the time actually spent. The co-relation is often absent that more work is necessarily perceived as valuable work, hence in studying perceptions, the disjunction has to be taken into account of. Time allocation studies are useful to demonstrate precisely this issue: while facts show that women work longer than men, it is simply not accounted for as work. As has been found in other time use studies carried out in South Asia, women spend more time working than men. In such a context, the most reliable means of capturing women's work pattern is a time allocation study, because it does not depend on any prior definition of work. Such data, which determine the actual time involvement in the expanded economic activities and conventional domestic activity, alone can reflect the actual participation of the women's work.

K Saradamoni has presented data on women cultivators and labourers in Kerela, Tamil Nadu and West Bengal. It is typical to find that the cultivators supervised work both within and outside the home. Apart from 'domestic' work, they also worked along with labourers in the field, looking after their employment and payment of wages when the husband was not present. Those who had very little land worked on others' farms as wage labour in addition to this in order to supplement their income (Saradamoni, 1988). Further, there are various supplementary tasks that women perform towards the process of agricultural production. In preparing food for the workers, taking food for other family members who may be in the fields, recruiting labourers and negotiating their terms, women are directly involved in the entire process.

Women's time allocation patterns in a study of two villages in Andhra Pradesh once again affirms that women actually spend more hours in work than males. Studying time allocation patterns for various activities such as crop production, animal husbandry, building and construction work, trading, marketing, transportation, domestic work, fuel gathering, food processing and all other social and religious obligations for each worker in the household, it was found that in all categories, women worked longer hours daily, than males (Sudha et al., 1993). In her study of some villages in Andhra Pradesh, Miesagain brings out the fact that in one of the villages which had a mix of women agricultural labourers and cultivators, 96 per cent of the women workers are engaged in agricultural work, while the corresponding figure for men is 65 per cent (Mies, 1987).[4]

These studies bring out the unreliability of official data, and the fact that in most cases the actual level of female participation in agriculture is higher. Studies indicate that the available macro-level data sets seriously underestimate the role of the women in India's household based, subsistence and semi-subsistence agriculture. One such study, by the ILO, shows that by expanding from the narrower definition and using a simplified activity schedule instead of the standard 'yes' or 'no' questions, the labour force participation rates for the same sample of rural women in central India varied from 3 per cent to 90 per cent (Anker et al., 1993). This strongly suggests that there are very few rural women in India who are not in some sense 'farmers', that is, working as wage labourers, unpaid workers in the family farm enterprise, or some combination of the two.

In order to fully understand the exact nature and extent of women's work participation in rice cultivation it is helpful to consider the division of tasks in the range of operations. It is generally true to say that where there are operations to be carried out using machines or animals, these are done by men, and most work which requires direct manual labour is done by women. There are few tasks performed by both men and women in the same way. Generally, men are responsible for preparing the field by ploughing and then levelling the field. They are also responsible for digging of wells and the small irrigation canals that run between the fields and making the bunds around the fields. Women 'help' in these by putting the mud from the canals on the bunds, or removing stones and the like from the fields. Men also

---

4   In their study of villages in two Haryana districts, Malit Kaur, et al. find that the average working day for women works out to be 13.2 h. Farm work took up the maximum time, with an average of 2.6 h, and food preparation and kitchen related work took up an average of 2.4 h. The main activities within this was cooking and fetching water. Cleanliness of the house took up an average of 2.1 h a day, and looking after animals 1.8 h on average. Laundry, sewing, and so on, child care and processing of food grains for cooking took up 1.4 h, 1.4 h and 1 h respectively. In this study, about 59.1 per cent of the respondents said that they did not get any leisure time (Kaur et al., 1988). Similar results are found in another study of Haryana by Munjal et al. (1988).

irrigate the fields before and after transplantation by drawing water from the wells with animals, or with the help of a simple lever system using a long bamboo shaft with a tin container usually attached at the end.

Women's role is to fertilize the fields with cow and buffalo dung before the actual planting of the seeds This is done manually in most cases as they also clear the seed beds of stones, and so on. When the rice plant has grown to its required height, transplantation is undertaken. This process requires that each individual sapling be handled separately, and is the most labour intensive part of rice cultivation. Weeding is also done exclusively by women, and like transplantation, involves no tools but is completely manual. The work in transplanting and weeding is particularly strenuous as it involves bending down to do the work for the entire time.

Though harvesting is done by both men and women, men are responsible for the threshing by driving animals over the rice, while women do the winnowing by fanning the grain to remove the husk. The drying, cleaning and processing of the grain is also done by women. These include parboiling and drying of paddy and responsibility for storage and preparation for the next year's planting. Women also prepare rice as storables in the form of puffed and flattened rice which can be consumed throughout the year. In addition, women perform the 'supportive' tasks such as taking meals for other family members to the fields and the preparation of meals for hired labour.

Notwithstanding this large and varied amount of work done by women, the idea that men are the ones who do the 'harder' jobs remain. Ploughing, irrigation and work involving physical strength is considered more difficult in this division, and consequently, men are understood to do the more valued work.

Land to the Tiller: Women and Land Reforms in India

India, like most Asian countries, is characterized by a high population density and small farm size in the agricultural sector. The average farm size is between 2 and 4 hectares, and despite redistributive land reforms, the distribution of farm lands is severely unequal. Farms exceeding 10 hectares occupy about 25 per cent of the land. The rationale behind agrarian reform, as in many other countries, has been the desire to give the ownership of land to the tiller. In the search for ways to make the land more productive and the rural economy dynamic, it was sought, in addition to removal of intermediaries, to confer ownership rights to tillers who did not hitherto have ownership.

Within the range of issues encompassed by land reform, the focus of analysis for our purposes is the aspect of land distribution. Land distribution includes the distribution of land from households with landholdings higher than a stipulated upper limit to households owning little or no land, as well as the granting of ownership rights to current tillers. The literature dealing with the merits, success and failure of land reforms in India is vast. While it is true to say that it has been largely a story of the failure of land reforms (Jannuzi, 1994; Appu, 1996; Padhi, 1997) others argue for renewing the case for land reforms in South Asia (Quibria, 1995).

The case of land reform policy in India is used here to illustrate the absence of recognition of women as workers and contributors to agricultural production in their own right in policies of the state. Thus far, the problems regarding enumeration of women's work in statistical data have been discussed and it was argued that such problems are based upon a limited conception of what constitutes women's 'work'. Detailed aspects of women's activities gathered from time allocation studies bring out the discrepancies in official data and the reality of women's activities that constitute 'work'.

The case of land reforms policy illustrates the very process of non-allocation following as a direct result of non-recognition. Although land reforms were based on principles of redistributive justice (that there should be no concentration of land in the hands of a few), empowerment (the state should facilitate control to workers over the productive assets, most importantly land) and economic justice (workers in agriculture should have control over means of production to reduce severe indebtedness and poverty of a majority of the agrarian population), the principle of gender equity was not integrated. The consideration of who constituted the subject group of 'farmers' or 'tillers' or 'tenants' was premised upon the male as the active worker/producer, upon ignorance of the nature and extent of women's work, and lastly, of their contributions to the family's survival as a result of such work. Further, where women are taken into account, they are again treated mainly as 'dependants' or non-contributors to family income (Agarwal, 1994, 1995).

The economic basis for the reforms has been the purported higher productivity of smaller plots of land. This higher productivity is a direct consequence of the intensive use of family labour on small farms, where there is a differential in costs in using family labour and hired labour within a dual labour market arising out of the prospect of unemployment for the latter (Quibria, 1995). As studies in the previous section have documented, women's role, particularly in supervision of tasks on family farms is significant. Agarwal (1994) also argues that supervision of hired labour is so important that it is entrusted only to family members. Even if large and small farms have families of equal size, the small farms clearly have more supervisors per acre, and hence can engage more profitably in labour – intensive cultivation. This labour input, as the various studies discussed earlier have shown, comes largely from women.

All the above notwithstanding, gender issues within land reforms have been virtually ignored. As Quibria flatly acknowledges,

> ... We know very little about the impact of land reform on (the) issue, a fact that ought to give us pause ... faced by a lack of research directed specifically at the status of women under regimes of land reform, we are led to speculate on the status of women in peasant societies ... (Quibria, 1995, 142).

An analysis of land reforms from a gendered perspective clearly shows that women are absent as the target of desired goals and objectives. Although officials with whom I spoke on the issue assured me that all leases and allocations under the land reform regulations presently were issued jointly to both spouses, men appear to continue as beneficiaries in greater number than women. In Sundargarh District as of the end of 1995, for example, while only 11 women had been granted leases under the Orissa Land Settlement Act 1959, the number for men was more than double at 29. Similarly, 35 women, as opposed to 72 men, were allocated land under the Orissa Land Reforms Act 1962 within the period 1990–1995.[5]

Further, land ceiling laws in many states explicitly overlook and ignore women as beneficiaries, in fact treating the female as a 'dependent', without entitlement to consideration as an independent unit. For example, in determining the fixation of ceiling for a 'family', the persons taken into consideration are the cultivator, his/her spouse, minor sons and unmarried minor daughters (Agarwal, 1995, 1994). Moreover, adult sons receive special consideration, either allowing additions to be made to the total land to be owned by the household, or, as entitled to hold a specified amount of land in their own right. As Agarwal notes,

> … Underlying the ceiling specification is clearly the assumption that those who are recognised either as part of the family unit or separately (as with adult sons) will be maintained by the land allowed …. Under these enactments we thus have the extraordinary situation where most states do not give any consideration, when fixing ceilings, for the maintenance needs of unmarried adult daughters and married minor daughters, while giving consideration to all sons, whatever their age or marital status … (emphasis added) (Agarwal, 1994, 219; 1995: A46).

Clearly, the inclusion of only unmarried minor daughters is based upon the presumption that a daughter who is married is to be considered within her husband's household. But what of the adult daughter who remains unmarried? What is the allocation of land for her maintenance? In addition to a gross inequality being created, the result is also the perpetuation of notion that the daughter is a 'burden' to her parents, while the son maintains the resource-total (or indeed, causes addition to it) of the family. The non-consideration of females within land reform laws is again explicit in the manner in which land is assessed for ceiling. In most cases, the holdings of both the spouses (where the wife also holds separate title to land) are aggregated in the assessment, while typically, it is in consultation with the husband alone that the decision is made as to whose portion of the aggregate will be declared surplus.

In considering law as culture, where law enshrines, and legitimates and reinforces basic societal values, and in its reforming aspect where it is an agent for spearheading cultural change, the land reform laws may be seriously brought into question on the issue of increasing gendered access to land. If one considers the potential of law to engender new values, and generate changed expectancies and attitudes (Baxi, 1986), land reform laws entirely missed the opportunity to foster more gender equitable values, ideas and symbols at best, and at worst, deepen the already deep-rooted notions of women as unproductive persons who play no significant role in the family or nation's economy as producers or workers in agriculture; as dependants liable to be 'maintained' by the husband's resources and ultimately, burdens to their parents if unmarried.

---

5   Official communication received from Tehsildar of Sundargarh District.

Conclusion

That women's role in agricultural production is overlooked and undervalued in the legal framework is only a reflection of the situation in official and public accounts and policy. The necessity to detail the extent of women's work in this area, and therefore to attempt an understanding of the major role that they play in the agricultural production arises from the fact that most women do not actually control the land. The problem therefore is that the control over land by women must be increased in order that they are considered in policy as major actors in agricultural production, not merely 'supportive' ones.

It is apparent from various studies that there is gross underestimation of women's work participation, especially in agriculture, where they in fact play a significant role. This is especially true of wage labourers who, generally being the poorest section of the society, are often the mainstay of their family's welfare, and of small and marginal peasant women, whose work is particularly difficult to evaluate in terms of the contribution to family income and resources. In the case of landless labourers, women's income is a major contribution to household income – essential for survival – even where wage rates for women are lower than for males. This fact cannot be emphasized enough because the conventional development theory often assumes that even when Indian women work in agriculture, their income is largely supplementary to that of the males in the households (Mencher, 1993).

Nonetheless, all the studies also point out that women in fact lack any control over the inputs to agricultural production such as land, institutional credit, education and training in farming methods, and so on. The first step in my view is to recognize that women are in fact significant contributors in agricultural production. Enhancing and supporting women in this role will allow for better access to the necessary inputs for growth. This in turn will provide the basis for women to negotiate control of the primary resource, land, by enabling a starting point from which women can in fact make decisions regarding resource allocation within their families due to increased recognition of their contribution and hence increased legitimacy of their demands.

It has also been argued (Basu, 1990) that in order to analyse the agrarian structure and its role in development, it is necessary to take into account other non-economic factors such as interpersonal beliefs that prevail in the community, the nature of land tenure and the structure of property rights. Speaking of the role of the interpersonal esteem is society, Basu points out that how hard people work, and whether they try and innovate must be understood in terms of their social status accorded to those activities in a particular society.

The invisibility of home-based work is tied to a general neglect of the household economy and a narrow definition of work which precludes its inclusion in official statistics. Considerable overlap may exist between the household and extra-household work, the former expanding to use up extrahousehold work time during special or crisis occasions, and the latter expanding to encroach upon household work time during peak agricultural periods. The household work sphere also expands whenever needed to include extra-household work that is income substitution, referred to as 'status production work' (Sharma and Singh, 1993).

Recognition of women's 'work' as inclusive of the range of women's tasks is therefore central to the dominant conception of 'work', gender roles within the society and the cultural ideology which determine such roles.

In the case of women and ownership of land within the agrarian sector, a gendered access to land requires law to create a basis of legitimacy on two counts: cultural as well as socio-economic. A gender equitable land reform policy could endow hitherto landless female agricultural labourers with ownership of land as well as consolidate the ownership of those with titles to land. However, once the land is legally within a woman's right to ownership, the land is likely to fall within the resource base of the household collectively, and the issue then becomes one of women's ability to bargain for the resource within the household.

The perceptions of legitimacy, based upon perceptions of contributions of women working in agriculture, by both women as well as society at large, are crucial therefore in two aspects. First, a recognition of the work and contribution of women in agriculture, and as producers in their own right, not merely dependants, or in supportive roles, would have the direct effect of greater gender equality within land reforms. Secondly, such recognition, in the policy framework of the state in its developmental policies generally, and the legal framework in particular, can lead to the greater effectiveness of law in its effort to create new values and ideas, in particular that of Hindu women's ownership of land. The effect of gendered land ownership, sought to be achieved in particular through the Hindu Succession Act is dependent in part, to the creation of a new basis of legitimacy through recognition of women's contribution to and role in agriculture at the same time that the hitherto entrenched cultural ideology that excludes them must be replaced by new values.

Chapter 7

Conclusion

> We cannot speak of helping women to stand on their own feet if we do not think of ways women can have access to and control over money, land and house. The first step is to reject the gift system and ask for a share in the family property. A woman should overcome the feeling that the home she shares with her husband is not hers. Secondly, legally speaking she should inherit and also be the joint owner of her husband's property because she too puts in her labour ('The Rural Women's Liberation Movement', in Gandhi and Shah, 1992, 243).

The legal rights guaranteed to Hindu women to independent ownership in a share of family property have by and large not been exercised by them (Sharma, 1989; Agarwal, 1994; Devi, 1994). Although the statutory changes, codified in the Hindu Succession Act 1956 have been in force for many decades, this non – exercise of rights is evidence of more fundamental problems with legal efforts to empower women and further gender equality. This book provides a deeper understanding of the factors that may contribute to this. A clearer understanding of the specific beliefs, ideologies, material and social structures which inform women's life-worlds and constitute their particular location, needs to be the starting point for a critical evaluation of law's effectiveness.

In order to address Hindu peasant women's ability to claim land, the analysis of law must take account of their particular locations and the constitutive realities of their lives. This means, in the context of Hindu peasant women, the need to address them both as Hindu women *and* peasant women. Whereas the legal regime establishes their claim to independent ownership as a right, legal and policy changes need to take account of their interests as the basis for establishing their claim to land ownership. Further, in so far as the institution of the 'right' focuses on their identity as Hindu women and locates their claim within the family, the parameters of such a right are constructed by principles within religious ideology both by statute and judicial pronouncements as well as in the normative understandings which inform Hindu women's lives in rural areas. In addition, addressing them as peasant women, whose claim to land ownership is located within the household, enables us to take account of their role as workers and producers in agricultural production as a constitutive aspect of their lives as peasants. This provides the basis upon which we can evaluate their interest in land ownership and analyse the particular ways in which such interest is impacted upon by the constitutive aspects of their lives as Hindu peasant women in rural India.

The bargaining approach, particularly as developed by Sen and Agarwal, allows for the analysis of the interaction between the ideological and material conditions that impact upon such access. In addition, it provides a broader perspective to address rural women's claim to land ownership, within their realities as Hindu peasant women in small farming households, and enables us to take account of the norms and processes that affect their access to resources. Drawing upon responses from Hindu peasant women gained through field research in Western Orissa, this book addresses two aspects as they operate to determine their bargaining position: perceptions of self-interest (particularly in the interest to own land independently) and perceptions of contributions (through work and production in agriculture).

In the field study, women have unambiguously expressed their reluctance, as Hindu women, to substantiate their claim to parental property through succession. Their identification with their roles as mothers, daughters and sisters is informed by the Hindu religious ideology to which they subscribe. Their roles as mothers, sisters and daughters is predicated upon the identification of their interest with their (husband's) family on the one hand, and separation from the natal family on the other. The consequence of this is the preclusion of their individual self-interest, where such preclusion is reinforced due to the acknowledged non-membership of a Hindu female within her natal family. Further, while there is a separation of their interest from their natal family, the very separation is predicated upon religious ideology positing females' exclusion from independent property ownership. In this case, therefore, the existence of an interest separate from the natal family does not lead to an expression of that interest in terms of independent property ownership of their share through succession. *Independent* ownership of land through succession to parental property therefore cannot be assumed to be a significant element of self-interest in the case of Hindu women.

Analysis of the legal framework promoting their right to land, particularly through the HSA, shows the extent to which law in fact reflects these ideological standpoints. This may be seen in two respects. First, both an evaluation of the statute and judicial decisions on various aspects of Hindu Law establish that law reaffirms constitutive aspects of Hindu women's roles and identities which exclude their claim to land. Second, in so far as the right to Hindu women's ownership of property is a change introduced by the law, which in fact contravenes their role and position which predicates their exclusion from property, there appears to be a co-existence of contradictory propositions established by law. In this, the right to ownership is effectively overcome by law's simultaneous reaffirmation of Hindu women's traditionally constituted roles.

The ideological background of the legal framework in post-independent India reveals the construction of 'Hindu' women and their right to ownership through succession within religious discourse. To the extent that Hindu law has been, and remains, founded upon the dominance of religion as the organizing principle to a significant extent, the efforts to address the particular issue of females' property rights have been bound by the tension to retain, embody and reflect the overall structure and premises of traditional Hindu law, as well as the attempt to change particular aspects within it, predominantly by introducing females' shares to parental property through succession.

The HSA embodies this tension. The retention of the Mitakshara coparcenary reiterates the fundamental division drawn within traditional Hindu law between males and females in respect of property rights. The continuance of this is antithetical to females' proprietary rights, yet this is precisely where the law attempts to locate its introduction of females' right to independent ownership of property. The ambiguity expressed by women presented in Chapter 4, clearly reflect the lack of legitimacy of females' rights to parental property within the traditional family structure. To the extent this structure corresponds to the underlying framework of the Hindu family upheld by the law, it overrides the effect of the introduced changes.

In evaluating women's self interest in land ownership, it would be difficult to conclude that the law, both in its statutory expression, as well as religious and cultural norms, fosters such an interest. Changes in the legal provisions affirming women's equal right to inheritance in the parents' property are based on largely false assumptions of the cultural and social reality of Hindu women in India.

The first assumption which is wrongly made is that Hindu women construct their personhood independent of her relations to others in the family. Secondly, it wrongly assumes that it as a matter of course that a Hindu woman continues to identify herself and be identified by others, as a member of her parents' family even after marriage. The next presumption that she can therefore have a legitimate expectation from her natal family follows from this. Further, the legal changes are also based upon the wrong assumption that many Hindu women, as sisters are willing to compete with brothers for the same interest in land, thereby jeopardizing their relations with brothers and any security they may expect thereby.

The assumptions upon which the law is based continue to be unrealized, and in this, the law itself plays a significant part, reinforcing the ideology that excludes such self-interest. Hindu cultural ideology establishes the normative force of women's subservient, dependent and familial role. The internalization of the norms by women, combined with the perpetuation of Hindu norms by law and the courts strengthen their operation to the extent that there is very limited scope for the emergence of women's interests as individuals and independent of relations to others. Although the reformative aspects in legal provisions are aimed at changing this to some extent, the legal provisions in fact operate to negative the impact, by incorporating and promoting those very aspects of women's position and social role that militate against it. The application of law by the courts shown through the examples of cases reinforces this.

The introduction of females' equal rights to succession in Hindu law is inadequate to strengthen Hindu women's bargaining position. The legal framework in fact strengthens the lack of females' individual self-interest to claim a share in parental property. The resulting position is one where the law, although it seeks to enhance Hindu women's independent ownership of land, by its very framework ultimately serves to perpetuate women's inability to own land.

The context of law must take account of the material aspects of women's lives in addition to the ideological, where analyses of gender and property have shown the two to be inextricably intertwined. A pluralistic approach to the analysis of law brings a broader perspective for the critical study of law's scope and domain, allowing both for the evaluation of the impact of religious norms upon women's lives, as well as the expansion of legal analysis within the household and the workplace. Applied to the context of this study, it makes clear women's legal entitlements are shaped to a significant extent by norms and values that are not necessarily given due recognition within official legal frameworks and processes. It highlights the critical need to take account of the totality of structures and processes, informed by a variety of norms and insists on the need to contextualize law and take account of women's lives as they are actually lived.

Whereas the issue of Hindu women's right to property has been framed by law in exclusively ideological terms, the critically important role of land in a predominantly subsistence driven agricultural context underscores the material significance of any ideological, religious or legal structures for those living within these. Thus, the conditions of being a Hindu on the one hand and the experience of being a peasant who is female as wife, sister, mother, and so on must be understood as necessarily being in engagement and being shaped by each other. To study women's access to property, where the subject position occupied by women is plural, multifaceted, representative of often reinforcing and sometimes opposing constructs and values calls for a more complete evaluation of the factors that make up that plurality, and therefore to evolve an understanding of law which has a broader frame of vision. Broadening the scope of analysis to incorporate Hindu peasant women's role in agricultural production is imperative to address their material realities as workers and producers, and essential to strengthening the basis of their interest in land ownership. In addition to an evaluation of their self-interest as it is determined by religious ideology and law's perpetuation of the same, the effect of perceptions of their contribution upon their ability to claim land ownership and the impact of law in reflecting such perceptions needs to be seriously considered.

Whereas the liberal principles of the legal and constitutional framework enable formal guarantees of equality, they also operate to exclude actual inequalities from the realm of the law. There is a division maintained between family/work, analogous to the public/private distinction implicit within liberalism. This serves on the one hand, to reinforce the operation of religious ideology in women's lives (within the 'private'), and to exclude from the purview of law the work that peasant women are engaged in (within the 'family').

The case of land reforms in India provides an example of law's non-recognition of women outside the 'private' sphere but in the 'public' domain. It illustrates law's unwillingness to recognize women's lives as determined not by religious ideology alone, but by their material conditions within subsistence agriculture as well. Although land reforms were based on principles of redistributive justice, empowerment and economic justice, these principles were deemed by law makers not to apply to women. In instituting a policy to transfer control of productive assets to the workers in order to alleviate the severe poverty of sections of the agrarian population, the assumption is that males constituted the subject group of 'farmers'. This was premised upon the assumption that the male is the active worker/producer, and the ignorance of the nature and extent of women's work.

The undervaluation of women's role in agricultural production in the legal framework is a reflection of the situation in official and public accounts and policy. The necessity to highlight women's role in agricultural production arises from the fact that most women do not actually control the land. The problem becomes circular: in so far as women are not considered to be significant to agricultural production, they are not given control over land, the productive asset; and to the extent they remain outside the category of landholders, they fall outside the purview of agricultural policy. A consideration of women as major actors in agricultural production, not merely 'supportive' ones within policy requires increased recognition of women's contribution to agriculture and greater control over the productive assets.

A precondition for the correction of the problem, therefore is to make this work visible through research and publications in order to help mobilize social and legislative action. In the event legislation does exist, as in the HSA and land reforms, the basis for creating new attitudes and expectations both on the part of women themselves and society in general, must be created in order to give effect to changes envisaged within the legislative efforts. Thus, access to land must be given primacy in applying the HSA, while the land reform laws must fully address and include women. The role of women themselves in making this effective must be highlighted through education and information. As shown in discussions throughout this book, socio-cultural values construct and define women's particular roles and position as Hindu women regarding various aspects of life, but particularly in relation to ownership of property. That the normative force of these values, derived from religion, results in an ideological framework which excludes them from having a claim upon land, particularly that belonging to the parents, is clearly a reality for many women. This needs to change.

The most recent changes in the Hindu Succession Act (Amendment) Act 2005 are a step in the right direction in setting up an equal basis of property ownership at birth. Whereas the inherent discrimination of the mitakshara system of exclusive male membership of the coparcenary has been formally overcome, the changes to the Act will not of themselves enable full equality in property ownership. As has been highlighted through this work, the *perceptions* of entitlement to property among Hindu women as well as wider society need to change. To the extent that the provisions of the HSA 1956 reflected the unequal positions of males and females within traditional Hindu Law, the recent changes have brought about greater equality by their removal. But to the extent that the provisions only reflected deeply held views and values, their removal does not necessarily herald the end to those values. Ultimately, the issue is one of law's impact in people's everyday lives. If the values which order and inform peoples lives are not adequately addressed by law, changes to the law per se will have little impact, at least in the foreseeable future. To re-order the values of inequality and subordination which imbue women's and men's lives, the changes have to be deep and wide. Legal change, to the extent that it heralds such a change is necessary. However, social change is the more important; creating a new basis for legal legitimacy of a claim will only bring about the desired change if the social legitimacy is also established. To this end, programmes have to be developed and sustained.

The situation with regard to property belonging to the husband, however, is quite different. Women, even Hindu women, identify their interest with that of their (husband's) family. In its extreme form, such interest is often understood and expressed as completely eradicating the 'individual' defined exclusively of the family and only existing as totally subsumed within that of the family. However, women's membership within the husband's family, granted by Hindu norms, may operate to define their obligations but at the same time limit their interests, conceived as legitimate only in terms of the community of the marital family. To this extent, it precludes their legitimate individual self-interest to independent ownership of any valuable resource, particularly land. However, their awareness of the tenuous nature of their position within the husband's family also develops within women an alternative understanding that their *expectation* of security must be addressed to and should be met by that very family. Women are cognizant that their independent interests and substantiation of these through property ownership within the marital family *should* be accorded legitimacy. Thus, the psycho-social normativity required asserting and realizing the claim that they should be entitled to a share in their husbands' property not only as widows upon the husband's death, but during the entire period while the marriage subsists, clearly exists. Although it may be felt by many women that they do not currently have a legitimate claim to independently own a share in their husband's property under prevalent religious norms, it is nevertheless possible to *argue* for the legitimacy of such a claim. This brings out the need for law to incorporate this and develop a regime of marital property. There is a growing recognition of the need for such a regime in India but at present the debate is being structured by the needs and interests of women with access to formal labour markets, particularly as professionals.

To what extent can their significant role within the material structures of subsistence production and survival strategies provide for the basis upon which such legitimacy may be argued? Given that these women are fully aware of their role and contribution to agricultural production, through what processes may this be translated into establishing effective bases to promote their claim to land?

In the case of women and ownership of land within the agrarian sector, a gendered access to land requires law to create a basis of legitimacy on two counts: cultural as well as socio-economic. Perceptions of women's contributions, in that they affect perceptions of legitimacy of women's claim to land, are crucial in two aspects. First, recognition of the work and contribution of women in agriculture, and as producers in their own right, not merely dependants, or in supportive roles, would have the direct effect of greater gender equality within land reforms. Secondly, such recognition, in the policy framework of the state in its developmental policies generally, and the legal framework in particular, can lead to the greater effectiveness of law in its effort to create new values and ideas, in particular that of Hindu women's ownership of land. The effect of gendered land ownership, sought to be achieved in particular through the Hindu Succession Act is dependent in part, on the creation of a new basis of legitimacy through recognition of women's contribution to and role in agriculture at the same time that the hitherto entrenched cultural ideology that excludes them must be replaced by new values.

Thus, the cultural and social matrix within which they are located, and with which they identify, do not allow Hindu women qua Hindu women to exercise their right, albeit protected by law. There is a significant gap between their lived understandings and perceptions and those promoted by law; a gap that effectively negatives any significant intersection and interaction. Where there may be an intersection, it would most likely be through challenges brought to the courts, where the law in fact provides a site for subverting challenges to the normative socio-cultural order and understandings (Basu, 1999). However these would be the exceptions rather than the rule; moreover they are indicative of the power of law being used to defeat its expressed objective. On the other hand, to the extent that law may be powerful in setting up norms, ideologies and meanings in society, it may be seen to be reinforcing precisely those norms and frameworks that are based upon the exclusion of women.

The discussion of Hindu law as it has been constituted by colonial engagement, on one hand, and as it operates to reinforce the normative force of religious principles in women's lives on the other, has significance for arguments towards a Uniform Civil Code ('UCC') in India. Whereas there has been much discussion and demand for the enactment of a UCC, it must be asked, in the light of conclusions resulting from this debate: what may be the content of such a Code? Where the purpose of the Code would be towards removing religion as the basis of law (Parasher, 1997), the question is whether this would in fact be a realistic foundation of law? Where religious norms and precepts continue to meaningfully construct, social, economic, political and cultural structures within which many women are located, can a presumption to the contrary by law be valid (Menski, 2003)? Can law be reflective of and pertinent to women while simultaneously remaining non-cognizant of the normative force of religion in their lives?

On the other hand, this book has shown the difficulties of law adhering to religious principles while at the same time attempting to reform certain aspects within them, without establishing a basis that is meaningful to the people it addresses (Smith, 1963; Bilgrami, 1997). Again, where such a Code could provide the starting point for the disengagement of law from active engagement with religion, particularly in the multi-religious context of India, perhaps we need to explore further other principles that are relevant to people's lives (Thapar, 1985; Gandhi and Shah, 1992).

In this regard, the clear religious obligation upon parents to ensure her marriage is open to re-interpretation as a wider obligation to secure her future material, psychological and social happiness. In my view, the realities of contemporary life and its obvious demands in securing an adequate livelihood and status would require but a small step to translate the above obligation of parents into one for providing adequate education and health care for the daughter. This is only an extension of the understanding of obligations which most parents already feel towards their sons.

The legal processes for realizing women's claims must also be reworked so as to remove any psychological and social barriers to women in approaching the law. In the case of marital property rights, discussed earlier, for example, we need to enable women's claim and entitlement to such property without placing the obligation upon them to initiate a process of formal separation or partition. Instead, the charge upon the property, regardless the formal ownership registration, could clearly be made in the name of the wife (to the extent of her share). Her independent ownership/ title could be effected for such purpose, where the claim of the creditor, buyer or transferee has to be realized, in the case of transfer through sale, credit or gift (Patel, 2006).

A similar process of shifting the focus to recognize the daughter's/sister's psycho-social reservations while enabling her to overcome them, *without requiring a necessary confrontation on her part* is also possible. The active assertion of her claim to her share by the daughter would become unnecessary, and perhaps simultaneously mitigate the fear of endangering good relations with her family. While these steps may appear small, they can have far-reaching impacts on the ability of women to make independent decisions, as well as enhance their own entitlements.

> Given that land is very rarely bought or sold in rural areas, the value of the land is greatest as a source of credit, and arguably, would fulfil a significant need in the case of cultivators. In this situation, creating a lien over the property, which need not be demarcated in title and ownership until a transfer is to be effected, leads to a greater potential for its use by women. Both daughters and wives could use their (residuary) right to a share in the property fare more effectively than when required, as at present, to assert their claim in opposition to sanctioned beliefs and norms by which they live and to which they are subject (Patel, 2006, 1264).

On the issue of recognizing women's work, we have a concrete lead to follow from the women themselves. They believe that their work and contribution to agricultural production is significant, and argue for the recognition of their role as such. This leads us to explore the ways through which such recognition may be given. We need to explore the facilities that may be generated to women as workers, identify the areas in which this may be done. We need to explore and identify the means through which recognition of women's role in agriculture may be made and institutions and functionaries through whom action may be taken. A starting point could be the provision of rural credit on the basis of work participation by various agencies. This could be worked in conjunction with the earlier point made regarding land titles. We also need to explore the training and development programmes addressed to women as workers within agriculture.

One of the areas to consider is the regime of land reforms operative in India today. We need to address in greater depth the foundations of such a regime, and acquire deeper insights into the ways gender may form an integral part of our understanding. We need to address the assumptions underlying land reform policy regarding the nature of the family/household to whom land is allocated, that the interest of the wife is subsumed under that of the husband. Although officials with whom I spoke on the issue assured me that all leases and allocations under the land reform regulations presently were issued jointly to both spouses, men appear to continue as beneficiaries in greater number than women.

The issue of land ownership is a difficult one even when one considers only two factors such as caste and class in the Indian society. To introduce the gender aspect makes it more complex, since the entire gamut of economic, social, cultural, religious and political forces that make up the patriarchal ideology are brought into play. However, in my view, though land ownership is the issue where gender biased ideology comes into play, it is possible to separate the issue of economic empowerment from empowerment in socio-cultural and political terms as the starting point of the analysis in law's approach to the question. It is not possible to separate actual empowerment into these spheres as the outcome in reality. However, precisely because of the overwhelming power of land issues to exacerbate other issues of gender bias, it is necessary to find a starting point in law that includes a focus on land issues in their economic as well as ideological aspect.

In this discussion of rural women's claim to land in India, the insights from various disciplines have broadened the scope of law's purview. They have brought within the legal framework the possibility for analysis of the women's claim to land as not only ideologically constructed, but materially affected. In this, legal analysis comes closer to encompassing the totality of factors that affect the subjects to whom it is addressed. Although such an analysis would also lead to an acceptance of the limits of law in affecting people's lives, we need to recognize and deal adequately with the reality that the policy framework set out by law is a very powerful framework for inducing change and supporting change in other areas of state policy. The role of law in moving away from setting up religion as the basis of people's actions, could lead to an emphasis, even the encouragement, of addressing other fundamental values by which people live. By taking account of women within land reforms, for example, we can move towards a framework which legitimizes the recognition of women's work. As this book has tried to argue, this in turn can be the basis for cumulative change in the women's entitlements, including that of property rights, and greater overall equality. Law can spearhead this process. The challenge that exists is to develop ways in which law may do so.

Where rural women's claims to land may be brought within legal analysis to address them not only as 'Hindu' women but also peasant women, where their claim may be seen to arise not only within the structure of the 'family' as ideologically constructed, but in the household as affected by their work and contribution to agriculture, a legal framework may yet be created which constructs rural women's claim to land ownership effectively.

Bibliography

Abu-Lughod, L. (1993), *Writing Women's Worlds: Bedouin Stories* (Berkeley: California University Press).

Adelman, S. and Paliawala, A. (1993), 'Law and Development in Crisis', in Adelman, S. and Paliawala, A. (eds).

Adelman, S. and Paliwala, A., eds (1993), *Law and Crisis in the Third World* (London: Hans Zell Publishers).

Agarwal, B. (1985), 'Work Participation of Rural Women in Third World: Some Data and Conceptual Biases', *Economic and Political Weekly*, 20, 51–52, 155–164.

Agarwal B. (ed.) (1988a), *Structures of Patriarchy: The State, the Community and the Household in Modernising Asia* (London: Zed Books).

Agarwal, B. (1988b), 'Who Sows? Who Reaps? Women and Land Rights in India', *Journal of Peasant Studies*, 15(4), 531–581.

Agarwal, B. (1992), 'Rural Women, Poverty and Natural Resources: Sustenance, Sustainability and Struggle for Change', in Harriss, B., Guhan, S. and Cassen, R.H. (eds).

Agarwal, B. (1994), *A Field of One's Own: Gender and Land Rights in South Asia* (Cambridge: Cambridge University Press).

Agarwal, B. (1995), 'Gender and Legal Rights in Agricultural Land in India', *Economic and Political Weekly*, March, 25, 39–56.

Agarwal, B. (1997), 'Bargaining and Gender Relations: Within and Beyond the Household', *Feminist Economics*, 3(1), 1–51.

Agarwal, B. (2003), 'Gender and Land Rights Revisited: Exploring New Prospects Via the State, Family and Market', *Journal of Agrarian Change*, 3, 1–2, January and April, 184–224.

Agarwala, R.K. and Ramanamma, A. (1994), 'Women and the Family Law', in Sarkar, L. et al. (eds).

Ahmed-Ghosh, H. (1993), 'Agricultural Development and Work Pattern of Women in a North India Village', in Bagchi, D. et al. (eds).

Alavi, H. and Harris, J., eds (1989), *Sociology of 'Developing Societies': South Asia* (London: Macmillan).

Alridge, J. et al., eds (1991), *Rethinking: Feminist Research Processes Reconsidered, Feminist Praxis* (Manchester: Sociology Department, Manchester University).

Altekar, A.S. (1991), *The Position of Women in Hindu Civilisation* (New Delhi: Motilal Banarasidas Publications Pvt Ltd).

Anandalaxmi, S. (1986), 'Is There a Psychology of Women', in Krishnaraj, M. (ed.).

Anker, R. et al. (1993), 'Methodological Issues in Collecting Time Used Data for Female Labour Force', in Sharma, A. and Singh, S. (eds).

Appu, P.S. (1996), *Land Reforms in India: A Survey of Policy, Legislation and Implementation* (New Delhi: Vikas Publishing House).

Bagchi, D. (1993), 'The Household and Extrahousehold Work of Rural Women in a Changing Resource Environment in Madhya Pradesh, India', in Bagchi, D. and Raju, S. (eds).

Bagchi, D. and Raju, S. (1993), 'In Sum and Looking Beyond: Suggestions for Future Research', in Bagchi, D. and Raju, S. (eds).

Bagchi, D. and Raju, S., eds (1993), *Women and Work in South Asia: Regional Patterns and Perspectives* (London: Routledge).

Bagchi, J., ed. (1995), *Indian Women: Myth and Reality* (Hyderabad: Sangam Books India Limited).

Bagwe, A. (1995), *Of Woman Caste: the Experience of Gender in Rural India* (London: Zed Books).

Baird, R.D., ed. (1993), *Religion and Law in Independent India* (Delhi: Manohar Publishers).

Bakshi, P.M. (1995), *The Constitution of India: Selective Comments* (Delhi: Universal Book Traders).

Banerjee, N. (1995), 'Sexual Division of Labour: Myths and Reality in the Indian Context', in Bagchi, J. (ed.).

Banks, J.A. (1957), 'The Group Discussion as an Interview Technique', *Sociological Review*, 5(1), 75–84.

Bardhan, K. (1985), 'Women's Work, Welfare and Status: Forces of Tradition and Change in India', *Economic and Political Weekly*, 20(50), 2207–2269.

Bardhan, P. (1984), *Land, Labor and Rural Development: Essays in Development Economics* (New York: Columbia University Press).

Barnett, H. (1997), *Sourcebook on Feminist Jurisprudence* (London: Cavendish Publishing Ltd.).

Barnett, H. (1998), *Introduction to Feminist Jurisprudence* (London: Cavendish Publishing Limited).

Basu, D.D. (1983), *Commentary on the Constitution of India* (Bombay: Tripathy).

Basu, K. (1990), *Agrarian Structure and Economic Underdevelopment* (London: Harwood Academic Publishers).

Basu, O. (1999), 'Cutting to Size: Property and Gendered Identity in the Indian Higher Courts', in Rajan, R. and Sunder (eds).

Baxi, U. (1986), 'What Kind of Agenda for Gender Justice', in Krishnaraj, M. (ed.).

Baxi, U. (1986), *Towards a Sociology of Indian Law* (New Delhi: Satvahan Publications).

Bayefsky, A.F., ed. (1988), *Legal Theory Meets Legal Practice* (Edmonton: Academic Publishers).

Beneria, L. (1988), 'Conceptualizing the Labour Force: The Underestimation of Women's Economic Activities', in Pahl, R.E. (ed.).

Beneria, L., ed. (1982), *Women and Development: The Sexual Division of Labour in Rural Societies* (Geneva: International Labour Organization).

Benholdt, Thomsen, V. and Mies, M. (1999), *The Subsistence Perspective: beyond the Globalised Economy* (London: Zed Books).

Bennholdt-Thomsen, V. (1981), 'Subsistence, Production and Extended Reproduction', in Young, K., Wolkowitz, C. and McCullagh, R. (eds).

Bentzon, W. et al. (1998), *Pursuing Grounded Theory in Law: South-North Experiences in Developing Women's Law* (Oslo: Tano Aschehoug).

Berik, G. (1996), 'Understanding the Gender System in Rural Turkey: Fieldwork Dilemmas of Conformity and Intervention', in Wolf, D.L. (ed.).

Beteille, A. (1991), 'Society and Politics in India: Essays in a Comparative Perspective', (London and Atlantic Highlands: The Athlone Press).

Bhagwati, P.N. (1993), 'Religion and Secularism Under the Indian Constitution', in Baird, R.D. (ed.).

Bhattacharya, S. (1985), 'On the Issue of Underenumeration of Women's Work in the Indian Data Collection System', in Jain, D. and Bannerji, N. (eds).

Bilgrami, A. (1997), 'Secular Liberalism and Moral Psychology of Identity', *Economic and Political Weekly*, October, 4, 2527–2540.

Blackden, C.M. and Morris-Hughes, E. (1993) 'Paradigm Postponed: Gender and Economic Adjustment in sub-Saharan Africa' (World Bank Report).

Blumberg, R.L. (1989), 'Toward a Feminist Theory of Development', in Wallace, R.A. (ed.).

Boserup, E. (1970), *Women's Role in Economic Development* (London: Allen & Unwin).

Bottomley, A. et al. (1987), 'Dworkin; Which Dworkin?', in Fitzpatrick, P. and Hunt, A. (eds).

Bourque, S.C. and Warren, K.B. (1990), 'Access Is Not Enough: Gender Perspectives on Technology and Education', in Tinker, I. (ed.).

Brown, J. et al. (2002), *Women's Access and Rights to Land in Karnataka* (Seattle: Report No), 114; Rural Development Institute.

Bruner, J. (1990), *Acts of Meaning* (Cambridge: Harvard University Press).

Bunch, C. and Carrillo, R. (1990), 'Feminist Perspectives on Women in Development', in Tinker, I. (ed.).

Burgess, R.G., ed. (1990), *Studies in Qualitative Methodology, Vol 2: Reflections on Field Experience* (London: Jai Press Inc).

Burgess, R.G., ed. (1991), 'Field Research: *A* Sourcebook and Field Manual', *Contemporary Social Science Research Series. 4* (New York: Routledge).

Chakrabarty, D. (1997), 'Postcoloniality and the Artifice of History: Who Speaks for "Indian" Pasts? in', Mongia, P. (ed.).

Chakravarti, U. (1990), 'Whatever Happened to the Vedic Dasi: Orientalism, Nationalism and a Script for the Past', in Sangari, K. and Vaid, S. (eds).

Chakravarti, U. (1998), *Rewriting History: the Life and Times of Pandita Ramabai* (New Delhi: Kali for Women).

Chandler, M. (1954), 'An Evaluation of the Group Interview', *Human Organization*, 13(2), 26–28.

Chanock, M. (1985), *Law, Custom and Social Order: the Colonial Experience in Malawi and Zambia* (Cambridge: Cambridge University Press).

Chatterjee, P. (1990), 'The Nationalist Resolution of the Women's Question', in Sangari, K. and Vaid, S. (eds).

Chatterjee, P. (1993), *Nationalist Thought and the Colonial World: A Derivative Discourse* (London: Zed Books).

Chaudhury, N.C. (1979), *Hinduism: A Religion to Live By* (London: Chatto & Windus).

Chaudhury, P. (1990), 'Customs in a Peasant Economy: Women in Colonial Haryana', in Sangari, K. and Vaid, S. (eds).

Chaudhury, P. (1993), 'Conjugality, Law and the State: Inheritance Rights as Pivot of Control in Northern India', in *Feminism and Law: NLSIU Journal* (eds).

Chhachhi, A. (1994), 'Identity Politics, Secularism and Women: A South Asian Perspective', in Hasan (ed.).

Chitnis, S. (1996), 'Feminism: Indian Ethos and Indian Convictions', in Ghadially, R. (ed.).

Chowdhry, G. (1995), 'Engendering Development? Women in Development (WID) in International Regimes', in Parpart, J.L. and Marchand, M.H. (eds).

Clay, E.J. and Schafer, B.B. (1984), *Room for Manoeuvre: An Exploration of Public Policy in Agriculture and Rural Development* (London: Heinemann).

Cottam, C.M. and Rao, S.V., eds (1993), *Women, Aid and Development* (Delhi: Hindustan).

Cotterell, R. (1992), *The Sociology of Law: An Introduction* (London: Butterworths).

Coward, H. (1993), 'India's Constitution and Presuppositions Regarding Human Nature', in Baird, R.D. (ed.).

Dahl, T.S. (1986), 'Women's Law: Methods, Problems and Values', *Contemporary Crises*, 10, 361–371.

Dak, T.M. and Sharma, M.L. (1988), 'Social Framework of Female Labour Participation on Rural Sector', in Dak, T.M. (ed.).

Dak, T.M., ed. (1988), *Women and Work in Indian Society* (Delhi: Discovery Publishing House).

Das, R.M. (1993), *Women in Manu's Philosophy* (Jalandhar: ABS Publications).

Datta, A. and Sinha, S. (1997), 'Gender Disparities in Social Well-Being: An Overview', *Indian Journal of Gender Studies*, 4(1), 51–65.

Davis, K. and Lijanaar, M. (1991), *The Gender of Power* (New Delhi; Sage Publications).

Derrett, J.D.M. (1968), *Religion, Law and the State in India* (London: Faber & Faber).

Derrett, J.D.M. (1970), *A Critique of Modern Hindu Law* (Bombay, N.M.; Tripathy Limited).

Derrett, J.D.M. (1978), *Essays in Classical and Modern Hindu Law – Vol. 4* (Leiden: E. J. Brill).

Desai, A.R. (1959), *The Social Background of Indian Nationalism* (Bombay: Popular Book Depot).

Dhagamwar, V. (1992), 'The Disadvantaged and the Law', in Harriss, B. et al. (eds).

Dixon, R. (1978), *Rural Women at Work: Strategies for Development in South Asia* (Baltimore: Johns Hopkins University Press).

Dixon, R. (1982), 'Women in Agriculture: Counting the Labour Force in Developing Countries', *Population and Development Review*, 8(3), 539–556.

Dixon-Mueller, R. (1985), *Women's Work in Third World Agriculture* (Geneva: ILO).

Dreze, J. and Sen, A. (1999), *India: Economic Development and Social Opportunity* (New Delhi: Oxford University Press).

Dror, Y. (1969), 'Law as a Tool of Directed Social Change: A Framework for Policy Making', in Dumont, L. (ed.) (1970) *Religion/Politics and History in India* (Paris: Mouton Publishers).

Dyson, T. and Moore, M. (1983), 'On Kinship Structure, Female Autonomy, and Demographic Behaviour in India', *Population and Development Review*, 9(1), 35–60.

Ehrlich, E. (1962), *Fundamental Principles of the Sociology of Law* (New York: Russell and Russell Inc.).

Eleonora, M. and Susan, S., eds (1991), *Women, Households and Change* (Tokyo: United Nations University Press).

Elson, D. (1991), *Male Bias in the Development Process* (Manchester: Manchester University Press).

Elson, D. and Pearson, R. (1981), 'The Subordination of Women and the Internationalisation of Factory Production', in Young, K. et al. (eds).

Engel, D.M. and Munger, F.W. (1996), 'Rights, Remembrance, and the Reconciliation of Difference', *Law and Society Review*, 30(1), 8–53.

Ferguson, K.E. (1988), 'Subject-Centredness in Feminist Discourse', in Jones, K.B. and Jonasdottir, A.G. (eds).

Finch, J. and Mason, J. (1990), 'Decision Taking in the Fieldwork Process: Theoretical Sampling and Collaborative Working', in Fitzpatrick, P. and Hunt, A. (eds) (1987) *Critical Legal Studies* (Oxford: Basil Blackwell).

Folbre, N. (1986), 'Hearts and Spades: Paradigms of Household Economics', *World Development*, 14(2), 245–255.

Fraser, N. (1989), *Unruly Practices: Power, Discourse and Gender in Contemporary Social Theory* (Cambridge: Polity Press).

Freeman, M. (1985), 'Towards a Critical Theory of Family Law', *Current Legal Problems*, 38, 153–187.

Friedman, L.M. and Macaulay, S. (1969), *Law and the Behavioural Sciences* (New York: The Bobbs-Merrill Company Inc).

Galanter, M. (1984), *Competing Equalities: Law and the Backward Classes in India* (Berkeley: University of California Press).

Gandhi, N. and Shah, N. (1992), *The Issues at Stake: Theory and Practice in the Contemporary Women's Movement in India* (New Delhi: Kali for Women).

Ganesh, K. and Carla, R. (1993), 'Gender: Between Family and State', *Economic and Political Weekly*, Vol. 23, October.

Gasper, D. (1993), 'Entitlements Analysis: Relating Concepts and Contexts', *Development and Change*, 24, 679–718.

Gasper, D. (1996), 'Culture and Development Ethics: Needs, Women's Rights, and Western Theories', *Development and Change*, 27, 627–661.

Gasper, D. and Staveren, K. (2003), 'Development as Freedom – and as what Else?' *Feminist Economics*, 9, 2–3, 137–161.

Gavigan, S. (1988), 'Law, Gender and Ideology', in Bayefsky, A.F. (ed.).

Gavigan, S. (1993), 'Paradise Lost, Paradox Revisited: The Implications of Familial Ideology for Feminist, Lesbian and Gay Engagement to Law', *Osgoode Hall Law Journal*, 31, 589–624.

Geertz, C. (1993), *Local Knowledge: Further Essays in Interpretive Anthropology* (London: Fontana Press).

Ghadially, R., ed. (1996), *Women in Indian Society: A Reader* (New Delhi: Sage Publications).

Gleason, S.E. (1991), 'Gender Bias in Estimating Female Labor Force Participation', in Scoville, J.G. (ed.).

Gledhill, A. (1964) *The British Commonwealth: The Development of its Law and Constitutions: India*, London.

Gluckman, M. and Devons, E. (1991), 'Procedures for Demarcating a Field Study', in Burgess, R. (ed.).

Goody, J. et al., eds (1976), *Family and Inheritance: Rural Society in Western Europe 1200–1800* (Cambridge: Cambridge University Press).

Government of India (1947), *Report of the Hindu Law Committee* (New Delhi: Government of India Press).

Government of India (1974), *Towards Equality: Report of the Committee on the Status of Women in India* (Department of Social Welfare) (New Delhi: Government of India Press).

Government of India (1993), *Statistical Profile on Women Labour (Fourth Issue)* (New Delhi: Ministry of Labour).

Government of India (1994), 'Area and Operational Holdings During 1990-91-Orissa', *Agricultural Census*, XXI, *Agricultural Situation in India*, 671–677.

Guhan, S. (1992), 'Social Security in India: Looking One Step Ahead', in Harriss, B. et al. (eds).

Gulati, L. (1978), 'Profile of a Female Agricultural Labourer', *Economic and Political Weekly*, March, 25, A-27–A-35.

Gupta, K.A. (1979), 'Travails of a Woman Fieldworker: A Small Town in Uttar Pradesh', in Srinivas, M.N. et al. (eds).

Harcourt, W., ed. (1997), *Feminist Perspectives on Sustainable Development* (London: Zed Books Ltd.).

Harding, S., ed. (1987), *Feminism and Methodology* (Milton Keynes: Open University Press).

Harris, B. et al., eds (1992), *Poverty in India: Research and Policy* (Bombay: Oxford University Press).

Harris, J.W. (2nd edn) (1997) *Legal Philosophies* (London: Butterworths).

Harris, O. (1981), 'Households as Natural Units', in Young, K. et al. (eds).

Harriss, B. (1990), 'The Intrafamily Distribution of Hunger', in Sen, A. and Dreze, J. (eds).

Hart, G. (1995), 'Gender and Household Dynamics: Recent Theories and their Implications', in Quibria, M.G. (ed.).

Hartmann, H.I. (1987), 'The Family as the Locus of Gender, Class and Political Struggle: The Example of Housework', in Hasan, Z. (ed.) (1994) *Forging Identities: Gender, Communities and the State in India* (New Delhi: Kali for Women).

Heimsath, C.H. (1964), *Indian Nationalism and Hindu Social Reform* (Princeton).

Heyzer, N. and Sen, G., eds (1994), *Gender, Economic Growth and Poverty: Market Growth and State Planning in Asia and the Pacific* (New Delhi: Kali for Women).

Hill, M.T. (2003), 'Development as Empowerment', *Feminist Economics*, 9(2–3), 117–135.

Hirschon, R. (1984), 'Property, Power and Gender Relations', in Hirschon, R. (ed.).

Hirschon, R., ed. (1984), *Women and Property – Women as Property* (New York: St. Martin's Press).

Hirshman, M. (1995), 'Women and Development: A Critique', in Parpart, J.L. and Marchand, M.H. (eds).

Honigmann, J.J. (1991), 'Sampling in Ethnographic Fieldwork', in Burgess, R. (ed.).

Indian Council of Social Science Research (1977), *Status of Women in India* (New Delhi: Allied Publishers).

Indian Council of Social Science Research (1988), *Status of Women in India: A Synopsis on the Report of the National Committee on the Status of Women (1971–74)* (New Delhi: ICSSR).

Indira Devi, M. (1994), 'Woman's Assertion of Legal Rights to Ownership of Property', in Sarkar, L. and Sivaramayya, B. (eds).

Jackson, C. (2003), 'Gender Analysis of Land: beyond Land Rights for Women?' *Journal of Agrarian Change*, 3(4), 453–480.

Jacobs, S. (1996), 'Structures and Processes: Land, Families and Gender Relations', *Gender and Development*, 4(2), 35–42.

Jacobs, S. (2002), 'Land Reform: Still a Goal Worth Pursuing for Rural Women?' *Journal of International Development*, 14, 887–898.

Jacobson, D. and Wadley, S.S., eds (1977), *Women in India* (New Delhi: Manohar).

Jain, D. and Banerjee, N., eds (1985), *Tyranny of the Household: Investigative Essays on Women's Work* (New Delhi: Shakti).

Jain, M.P. (1966), *Outlines of Indian Legal History* (Bombay: Tripathy).

Jaising, I. (2005), 'Unequal Reform', *Communalism Combat*, 11, 104. Available at http://www.sabrang.com/cc/archive/2005/jan05/gender.html, Accessed on: 15/2/06.

Jaising, I., ed. (1996) *Justice for Women: Personal Laws, Women's Rights and Law Reform* (Mapusa: The Other India Press).

Jalali, R. (1994), *Indian Women in the Smritis* (Jammu: Vinod Publishers and Distributors).

Jannuzi, F.T. (1994), *India's Persistent Dilemma: the Political Economy of Agrarian Reform* (Oxford: Westview Press).

Jaquette, J.S. (1990), 'Gender and Justice in Economic Development', in Tinker, I. (ed.).

Jayawardena, K. (1988), *Feminism and Nationalism in the Third World* (London: Zed Books).

Jayawardena, K. and de Alwis, M., eds (1996), *Embodied Violence: Communalising Women's Sexuality in South Asia* (London: Zed Books).

Jenkins, I. (1980), *Social Order and the Limits of Law: A Theoretical Essay* (Princeton: Princeton University Press).

Jha, U.S. et al., eds (1998), *Status of Indian Women: Crisis and Conflict in Gender Issues, Volume 1, Gender and Social Order* (New Delhi: Kanishka Publishers).

Jha, U.S. et al., eds (1998) *Status of Indian Women: Crisis and Conflict in Gender Issues, Volume 2, Progressive Women and Political Identity* (New Delhi: Kanishka Publishers).

Jhabvala, N.H. (ed.) (1993), *Principles of Hindu Law* (Bombay: C. Jamnadas and Co.).

Johnson, H.M., ed. (1978), *Social System and Legal Process* (London: Jossey-Bass).

Jonasdottir, A.G. (1988), 'On the Concept of Women's Interests, and the Limitations of Interest Theory', in Jones, K.B. and Jonasdottir, A.G. (eds).

Jones, K.B. and Jonasdottir, A.G., eds (1988), *The Political Interests of Gender: Developing Theory and Research with a Feminist Face* (London: Sage Publications).

Joseph, C. and Eswara Prasad, K.V., eds (1995), *Women, Work and Inequity: the Reality of Gender* (New Delhi: National Labour Institute).

Kabeer, N. (1994), *Reversed Realities: Gender Hierarchies in Development Thought* (London: Verso).

Kakar, S. (1996), 'Feminine Identity in India', in *Women in Indian Society: A Reader.* Ghadially, R. (ed.) (London: Sage Publications).

Kane, P.V. (1968) (2nd ed.), *A History of the Dharmasatras: Ancient and Medieval Religious and Civil Law* (Poona: Bhandarkar Oriental Research Institute).

Kapur, R. and Cossman, B., eds (1996), *Feminist Terrains in Legal Domains: Interdisciplinary Essays on Women and Law in India* (New Delhi: Kali for Women).

Kapur, R. and Cossman, R. (1996), *Subversive Sites: Feminist Engagements with Law in India* (London: Sage Publications).

Kaur, M. et al. (1988), 'Women and Work in Rural Society', in Dak, T.M. (ed.).

Kidder, R.L. (1978), 'Western Law in India: External Law and Local Response', in Johnson, H.M. (ed.).

Kline, M. (1994), 'The Colour of Law: Ideological Representations of the First Nations Legal Discourse', *Social and Legal Studies*, 3, 451.

Krishnaraj, M. and Chanana, K., eds (1989), *Gender and Household Domain: Social and Cultural Dimensions* (London: Sage Publications).

Krishnaraj, M., ed. (1986), *Women's Studies in India: some Perspectives* (Bombay: Popular Prakashan).

Krishnaswamy, S. (1996), 'Female Infanticide in Contemporary India: A Case Study of Kallars in Tamil Nadu', in Ghadially, R. (ed.)

Kumar, N. (1992), *Friends, Brothers and Informants: Fieldwork Memoirs of Banaras* (Berkeley: University of California Press).

Kynch, J. and Sen, A. (1983), 'Indian Women: Well-Being and Survival', *Cambridge Journal of Economics*, 7, 363–380.

Leslie, J. (Trans.) (1995), *The Perfect Wife* by Tryambakayajvan, Penguin Books.

Lim, L.Y.C. (1990), 'Women's Work in Export Factories: The Politics of a Cause', in Tinker, I. (ed.).

Mackintosh, M. (1981), 'Gender and Economics: The Sexual Division of Labour and the Subordination of Women', in Young, K. et al. (eds).

Madan, G.R. (1979), *Western Sociologists on Indian Society: Marx, Spencer, Weber, Durkheim, Pareto, and Kegan Paul* (London: Routledge).

Madan, T.N. (1994), 'The Structural Implications of Marriage in North India: Wife-Givers and Wife-Takers among the Pandits of Kashmir', in Uberoi, P. (ed.).

Mago, S.P. (1996), *Joint Property and Partition at a Glance* (Delhi: Vinod Publishing House).

Maguire, P. (1987), *Doing Participatory Research: A Feminist Approach* (Massachusetts: University of Massachusetts).

Mandelbaum, D.G. (1970), *Society in India, Vol. One: Continuity and Change* (Berkeley: University of California Press).

Mani, L. (1990), 'Contentious Traditions: The Debate on Sati in Colonial India', in Sangari, K. and Vaid, S. (eds).

Marchand, M.H. (1995), 'Latin American Women Speak on Development: Are We Listening Yet?', in Parpart, J.L. and Marchand, M.H. (eds).

Mathur, A. (1994), 'Work Participation, Gender and Economic Development: A Quantitative Anatomy of the Indian Scenario', *Journal of Development Studies*, 30(2), 466–504.

Maynard, M. (1994), 'Methods, Practice and Epistemology: The Debate about Feminism and Research', in Maynard, M. and Purvis, J. (eds).

Maynard, M. and Purvis, J., eds (1994), *Researching Women's Lives from a Feminist Perspective* (London: Taylor & Francis Ltd).

Mazumdar, V. (1976), 'The Social Reform Movement in India', in Nanda, B.R. (ed.).

Mazumdar, V. and Sharma, K. (1990), 'Sexual Division of Labor and the Subordination of Women: A Reappraisal from India', in Tinker, I. (ed.).

Mehdi, R. and Shaheed, F., eds (1997), *Women's Law in Legal Education and Practice in Pakistan* (Copenhagen: New Social Science) Monographs.

Mencher, J.P. (1989), 'Women Agricultural Labourers and Land Owners in Kerala and Tamil Nadu: Some Questions about Gender and Autonomy in the Household', in Krishnaraj, M. and Chanana, K. (eds).

Mencher, J.P. (1993), 'Women, Agriculture and the Sexual Division of Labour', in Bagchi, D. and Raju, S. (eds).

Menon, N. (1995), 'The Impossibility of "Justice": Female Foeticide and Feminist Discourse on Abortion', *Contributions to Indian Sociology*, 29(1–2), 369–392.

Menski, W. (2003), *Hindu Law: Beyond Tradition and Modernity* (New Delhi: Oxford University Press).

Merillat, H.C.L. (1970), *Land and the Constitution in India* (New York: Columbia University Press).

Merry, S.E. (1988), 'Legal Pluralism', *Law and Society Review*, 22(5), 869–896.

Messiah, J., ed. (1993), *Women in Developing Economies: Making Visible the Invisible* (Oxford: UNESCO).

Mies, M. (1980), *Indian Women and Patriarchy* (New Delhi: Concept Publishing Company).

Mies, M. (1982), *The Lace Makers of Narsapur: Indian Housewives Produce for the World Market* (London: Zed Books).

Mies, M. (1986), 'Indian Women in Subsistence and *Agricultural* Labour', *Women, Work and Development*, 12 (Geneva: ILO).

Mies, M. (1988), *Women: the Last Colony* (London: Zed Books).

Mitter, D.N. (1984), *The Position of Women in Hindu Law* (New Delhi: Inter-India Publications).

Mohan, G. (1997), 'Developing Differences: Post-Structuralism and Political Economy in Contemporary Development Studies', *Review of African Political Economy*, 73, 311–328.

Mohanty, C.T. (1991), 'Under Western Eyes: Feminist Scholarship and Colonial Discourses', in Mohanty, C.T. et al. (eds).

Mohanty, C.T. et al., eds (1991), *Cartographies of Struggle: Third World Women and the Politics of Feminism* (Bloomington, Ind.; University Press).

Molyneux, M. (1998), 'Analysing Women's Movements', *Development and Change*, 29, 219–245.

Momsen, J. and Kikiard, V., eds (1993), *Different Places, Different Voices: Gender and Development in Africa, Asia and Latin America* (London: Routledge).

Mongia, P., ed. (1997), *Contemporary Postcolonial Theory: A Reader* (Delhi: Oxford University Press).

Moore, H.L. (1991), *Feminism and Anthropology* (Cambridge: Polity Press).

Moore, H.L. (1995), *A Passion for Difference: Essays in Anthropology and Gender* (Cambridge: Polity Press).

Moore, S.F. (1978), *Law as Process: An Anthropological Approach* (London: Routledge).

Moser, C.O.N. (1993), *Gender Planning and Development: Theory, Practice and Training* (London: Routledge).

Mukherjee, P. (1978), *Hindu Women, Normative Models* (Calcutta: Orient Longman).

Mukhopadhyay, M. (1985), *Silver Shackles: Women and Development in India* (Oxford: Oxfam).

Mulla (1994), *Principles of Hindu Law*, Desai, S.T. ed. (Bombay: N. M. Tripathi Private Limited).

Munger, F. (1998), 'Immanence and Identity: Understanding Poverty through Law and Society Research', *Law and Society Review*, 32(4), 931–947.

Munjal et al. (1988), 'Work Participation and Time Allocation Pattern among Rural Women', in Dak, T.M. (ed.).

Murdoch, G.P. (1949), *Social Structure* (New York: Macmillan).

Naffine, N. and Owens, R.J., eds (1997), *Sexing the Subject of Law* (Sydney: Sweet & Maxwell).

Nagel, S. (1969), *The Legal Process from a Behavioural Perspective* (Homewood, Illinois: The Dorsey Press).

Nair, J. (1993), 'From Devadasi Reform to SITA: Reforming Sex Work in Mysore State, 1892–1937', *Feminism and The Law: NLSIU Journal*, 82–94.

Nair, J. (2000), *Women and Law in Colonial India: A Social History* (New Delhi: Kali for Women).

Nanda, B.R., ed. (1976), *Indian Women from Purdah to Modernity* (New Delhi: Vikas).

Narayan, V. (2001), *Gender and Community: Muslim Women's Rights in India* (Toronto: University of Toronto Press).

Natarajan, S. (1959), *A Century of Social Reform in India* (Bombay).

Nussbaum, M.C. (2003), 'Capabilities as Fundamental Entitlements: Sen and Social Justice', *Feminist Economics*, 9(2–3), 33–59.

O'Donovan, K. (1985), *Sexual Divisions in Law* (London: Weidenfeld & Nicolson).

O'Flaherty, W. and Derrett, J.D.M., eds (1983), *The Concept of Duty in Southern Asia* (New Delhi: Vikas).

Oakley, A. (1988), 'Interviewing Women: A Contradiction in Terms', in Roberts, H. (ed.).

Oldenberg, Veena, Talwar (1990) 'Lifestyles as Resistance: The Case of the Courtesans of Lucknow, India', *Feminist Studies* ,16: 2, 259–287.

Omvedt, G. (1994), 'Dependency Theory, Peasants and Third World Crisis', *Economic and Political Weekly*, January, 22, 169–176.

Padhi, S. (1985), 'Property in Land, Land Market and Tenancy Relations in the Colonial Period: A Review of Theoretical Categories and a Study of a Zamindari District', in Raj, K.N. et al. (eds).

Padhi, S. (1997), 'Looking Back on Land Reforms', *Economic and Political Weekly*, September, 20, 2394.

Pahl, R.E., ed. (1988), *On Work: Historical, Comparative and Theoretical Approaches* (Oxford: Basil Blackwell).

Panda, P.K. (1997), 'Female Headship, Poverty and Child Welfare: A Study of Rural Orissa', *Economic and Political Weekly*, October, 25, WS-73–WS-82.

Papanek, H. (1989), 'Family Status-Production Work: Women's Contribution to Social Mobility and Class Differentiation', in Krishnaraj, M. and Chanana, K. (eds).

Papanek, H. (1990), 'To Each Less Than She Needs, From Each More Than She Can Do: Allocations, Entitlements, and Value', in Tinker, I. (ed.).

Parasher, A. (1992), *Women and Family Law Reform in India: Uniform Civil Code and Gender Equality* (New Delhi: Sage Publications).

Parasher, A. (1997), 'Family Law as a Means of Ensuring Gender Justice for Indian Women', *Indian Journal of Gender Studies*, 4(2), 199–229.

Parpart, J.L. and Marchand, M.H., eds (1995), *Feminism/postmodernism/development* (London: Routledge).

Patel, R. (2000), 'Perceptions, Norms and Hindu Women's Property Rights in India – A Discussion of Legal Pluralism', in Stewart, A. (ed.), *Gender, Law and Social Justice* (London: Blackstone), 161–173.

Patel, R. (2002), 'Gender, Production and Access to Land: The Case for Female Peasants in India', in Parpart, J.L., Rai, S.M. and Staudt, K. (eds), *Rethinking Empowerment in a Global/Local World: Gendered Perspectives* (London: Routledge).

Patel, R. (2005), 'Women's Right to Property under Hindu Law: Gendered Entitlements and Traditional Obligations', *Indian Socio-Legal Journal*, XXXI, 73–94.

Patel, R. (2006), 'Hindu Women's Property Rights in India: a Critical Appraisal', *Third World Quarterly*, 27(7), 1255–1268.

Patel, V. (1996), 'Sex Determination and Sex Pre-Selection Tests: Abuse of Advanced Technologies', in Ghadially, R. (ed.).

Pateman, C. (1988), *The Sexual Contract* (London: Polity Press).

Pateman, C. and Grosz, E., eds (1986), *Feminist Challenges: Law and Social Theory* (Allen & Unwin).

Pathak, Z. and Rajan, R.S. (1989) 'Shah Bano', *Signs: Journal of Women in Culture and Society*, 14:3, 558–582.

Petersen, H. (1992), 'On Women and Legal Concepts: Informal Law and the Norm of Consideration', *Social and Legal Studies*, 1, 493–513.

Petersen, H. (1996), *Home Knitted Law. Norms and Values in Gendered Rule-Making* (Aldershot: Dartmouth).

Petersen, H. (1997), 'Legal pluralism and its Relevance for Women's Law', in Mehdi, R. and Shaheed, F. (eds).

Petersen, H. and Zahle, H., eds (1995), *Legal Polycentricity: Consequences of Pluralism in Law* (Aldershot: Dartmouth).

Pettigrew, J. (1988), 'Reminiscences of Fieldwork among the Sikhs', in Roberts, H. (ed.).

Podgo'recki, A. and Whelan, C.J., eds (1981), *Sociological Approaches to Law* (London: Croom-Helm).

Posner, R. (2004), *Frontiers of Legal Theory* (Cambridge: Harvard University Press).

Quibria, M.G., ed. (1995), *Critical Issues in Asian Development: Theories, Experiences and Policies* (Hong Kong: Oxford University Press).

Rai, S.M. (1999), 'Developing Explanations for Difference(s): Gender and Village-Level Democracy in India and China', *New Political Economy*, 4(2), 233–250.

Rai, S.M. (2002), *Gender and the Political Economy of Development* (Cambridge: Polity).

Raj, K.N. et al., eds (1985), *Essays on the Commercialization of Indian Agriculture* (Delhi: Oxford University Press).

Rajan, R.S., ed. (1999), *Signposts: Gender Issues in Post Independence India* (Delhi: Kali for Women).

Ramani Rao, S.V. et al. (1994), *Women at Work in India*, Vol. 2 (New Delhi: Sage Publications).

Ranadive, J.R. (1994), 'Gender Implications of Adjustment Policy Programme in India: Significance of the Household', *Economic and Political Weekly*, April, 30, WS-12–WS-18.

Rashid, R. and Quibria, M.G. (1995), 'Is Land Reform Passé? With Special Reference to Asian Agriculture', in Quibria, M.G. (ed.).

Rathgeber, E.M. (1995), 'Gender and Development in Action', in Parpart, J.L. and Marchand, M.H. (eds).

Razavi, S. (2003), 'Introduction: Agrarian Change, Gender and Land Rights', *Journal of Agrarian Change*, 3:1–2, January and April, 2–32.

Risseeuw, C. (1991), 'Bourdieu, Power and Resistance: Gender Transformation in Sri Lanka', in Davis, K. and Lijanaar, M. (eds).

Roberts, H., ed. (1988), *Doing Feminist Research* (London: Routledge).

Rose, N. (1987), 'Beyond the Public/Private Division: Law, Power and the Family', in Fitzpatrick, P. and Hunt, A. (eds).

Ross, H. (2001), *Law as A Social Institution* (Oxford: Hart Publishing).

Said, E. (1978), *Orientalism* (London: Routledge).

Sanday, P.A. (1973), 'Toward a Theory of the Status of Women', *American Anthropologist*, 75, 1683–1700.

Sangari, K. (1999), *Politics of the Possible: Essays on Gender, History, Narratives, Colonial English* (New Delhi: Tulika).

Sangari, K. and Vaid, S., eds (1990), *Recasting Women: Essays in Indian Colonial History* (Delhi: Kali for Women).

Santos, B.S. (1987), 'Law: A Map of Misreading. Toward a Postmodern Conception of Law', *Journal of Law and Society*, 14, 3.

Saradamoni, K. (1994), 'Progressive Land Legislations and Subordination of Women', in Sarkar, L. and Sivaramayya, B. (eds).

Sardamoni, K. (1988), 'Women Labourers, Women Cultivators and Contribution to Agriculture', in Dak, T.M. (ed.).

Sarkar, L. and Sivaramayya, B., eds (1994), *Women and Law: Contemporary Problems* (New Delhi: Vikas Publishing House).

Scoville, J.G., ed. (1991), *Status Influences in Third World Labor Markets: Caste, Gender and Custom* (Berlin: De Gruyter/Studies in Organization).

Sen, A. (1983), 'Economics and the Family', *Asian Development Review*, 1(2), 14–26.

Sen, A. (1987), 'Gender and Cooperative Conflicts', WIDER Working Papers, WP 18 July (UN: UN University).

Sen, A. (1990), 'Gender and Cooperative Conflicts', in Tinker, I. (ed.), *Persistent Inequalities: Women and World Development* (New York: Oxford University Press).

Sen, A. and Dreze, J., eds (1990), *The Political Economy of Hunger*, Vol. 1 (Oxford: Clarendon Press).

Sen, G. and Sen, C. (1985), 'Women's Domestic Work and Economic Activity', *Economic and Political Weekly*, 20(17), April 27, WS-49-56.

Sen, P.N. (1984), *General Principles of Hindu Jurisprudence* (Allahabad: Allahabad Law Agency).

Shah, A.M. (1974), *The Household Dimension of the Family in India* (Berkeley: University of California Press).

Shankar Jha, U. et al., eds (1998), *Status of Indian Women, Vol. 1* (New Delhi: Kanishka Publishers).

Sharma, A.N. and Singh, S., eds (1993), *Women and Work: Changing Scenario in India* (Delhi: B. R. Publishing House).

Sharma, I.C. (1965), *Ethical Philosophies of India* (London: George Allen & Unwin Co.).

Sharma, M. (1985), 'Caste, Class and Gender: Production and Reproduction in North India', *The Journal of Peasant Studies*, 12(4), 57–88.

Sharma, P. (1990), *Hindu Women's Right to Maintenance* (New Delhi: Deep and Deep Publications).

Sharma, U. (1984), 'Dowry in North India: Its Consequences for Women', in Hirschon, R. (ed.).

Sharma, U. (1989), 'Women, Work and Property in North-West India', in Alavi, H. and Harris, J. (eds).

Sharma, U. (1994), 'Dowry in North India: Its Consequences for Women', in Uberoi, P. (ed.).

Shiva Kumar, A.K. (1996), 'UNDP's Gender Related Development Index', *Economic and Political Weekly*, April, 6.

Shohat, E. (1997), 'Notes on the Post-Colonial', in Mongia, P. (ed.).

Siim, B. (1988), 'Towards a Feminist Rethinking of the Welfare State' in Jones, K.B. and Jonasdottir, A.G. (eds).

Simon, J.L. and Burstein, P. (1985), *Basic Research Methods in Social Science*, 3rd edn (New York: Random House).

Simon, R.J., ed. (1968) *The Sociology of Law: Interdisciplinary Readings* (San Fransisco: Chandler Publishing Company).

Singh, I. (1990), *The Great Ascent: the Rural Poor in South Asia* (London: Published for the World Bank) by Johns Hopkins Press.

Sinha, S.P. (1995), 'Legal Policentricity', in Petersen, H. and Zahle, H. (eds).

Sivaramayya, B. (1988), 'The Hindu Succession (Andhra Pradesh Amendment) Act 1985: A Move in the Wrong Direction', *Journal of the Indian Law Institute*, 30(2), 166–173.

Smart, C. (1984), *The Ties that Bind: Law, Marriage and the Reproduction of Patriarchal Relations* (London: Routledge).

Smart, C. (1989), *Feminism and the Power of Law* (London: Routledge).

Smith, D.E. (1963), *India as a Secular State* (London: Oxford University Press).

Smith, D.E. (1987), 'Women's Perspective as a Radical Critique of Sociology', in Harding, S. (ed.).

Somjee, G. (1989), *Narrowing the Gender Gap* (London: Macmillan Publishing).

Srinivas, M.N. (1967), *Social Change in Modern India* (Berkeley: University of California Press).

Srinivas, M.N. et al., eds (1979), *The Fieldworker and the Field: Problems and Challenges in Sociological Investigation* (Delhi: Oxford University Press).

Stewart, A. (1993), 'The Dilemmas of Law in Women's Development', in 'Law and Development in Crisis', in Adelman, S. and Paliawala, A. (eds).

Stuart, S.N., ed. (1969), 'Law and Social Change', *Contemporary Social Science*, 3 (London: Sage).

Subamma, M. (1992), *Hinduism and Women* (Delhi: Ajanta Publications).

Tamanaha, B.Z. (1993), 'The Folly of the "Social Scientific" Concept of Legal Pluralism', *Journal of Law and Society*, 20(2), 192–217.

Thapar, R. (1985), 'Secularism and Society', *Economic and Political Weekly*, XX(34), August 24, 1437–1438.

Tharu, S. (1995), 'Slow Pan Left: Feminism and the Problematic of Rights', in Bagchi, J. (ed.).

The World Bank (1992), 'Report on Gender and Poverty in India' (Washington, D.C.).

Thrift, N. (1996), *Spatial Formations* (London: Sage Publications).

Tinker, I. (1990), 'The Making of a Field: Advocates, Practitioners and Scholars', in Tinker, I. (ed.).

Tinker, I., ed. (1990), *Persistent Inequalities: Women and World Development* (New York: Oxford University Press).

Tong, R.P. (1998), *Feminist Thought: A More Comprehensive Introduction* (Oxford: Westview Press).

Treves, R. and van Loon, G. (1968), *Norms and Actions: National Reports on the Sociology of Law* (The Hague: Martinus-Nijhoff).

Uberoi, P. (1995), 'When Marriage Is Not a Marriage? Sex, Sacrament and Contract in Hindu Marriage', *Contributions to Indian Sociology*, 29, 1–2.

Uberoi, P., ed. (1994), *Family, Kinship and Marriage in India* (Delhi: Oxford University Press).

Udayagiri, M. (1995), 'Challenging Modernization: Gender and Development, Postmodern Feminism and Activism', in Parpart, J.L. and Marchand, M.H. (eds).

UNRISD (2005) *Gender Equality: Striving for Justice in an Unequal World*, Geneva.

Visvanathan, N. et al., eds (1997), *The Women, Gender and Development Reader* (London: Zed Books Ltd.).

Wadley, S. (1996), 'Women and the Hindu Tradition', in Ghadially, R. (ed.).

Wallace, R.A., ed. (1989), *Feminism and Sociological Theory* (London: Sage Publications).

Wallman, S., ed. (1979), *Social Anthropology of Work* (London: Academic Press).

Weber, M. (1958), *The Religion of India: the Sociology of Hinduism and Buddhism* (New York: The Free Press).

Whitehead, A. (1981), '"I'm Hungry, Mum": The Politics of Domestic Budgeting', in Young, K., Wolkowitz, C. and McCullaugh, R. (eds).

Whitehead, A. (1984), 'Women and Men; Kinship and Property: Some General Issues [1]', in Hirschon, R. (ed.).

Whitehead, A. (1990), 'Rural Women and Food Production in Sub Saharan Africa', in Sen, A. and Dreze, J. (eds).

Whyte, R.O. and Whyte, P. (1982), *The Women of Rural Asia* (Boulder: Westview Press).

Wieringa, S. (1994), 'Women's Interests and Empowerment: Gender Planning Reconsidered', *Development and Change*, 25(4), 829–848.

Wolf, D.L. (1996), 'Situating Feminist Dilemmas in Fieldwork', in Wolf, D.L. (ed.).

Wolf, D.L., ed. (1996), *Feminist Dilemmas in Field Work* (Oxford: Westview Press).

Woodman, G. (1997), 'Progress Through Complexity: Options for the Subjects of Legal Pluralism', in Mehdi, R. and Shaheed, F. (eds).

Young, K. et al., eds (1981), *Of Marriage and the Market* (London: CSE Books).

Young, K. et al., eds (1981), *Of Marriage and the Market: Women's Subordination in International Perspective* (London: CSE Books).

Zelditch, M., Jr (1991), 'Some Methodological Problems of Field Studies', in Burgess, R.G. (ed.), *Field Research: A Sourcebook and Field Manual*, Contemporary Social Science Research Series, 4, General Editor: Martin Bulmer (London and New York: Routledge).

Index